THE DOHA
ROUND TEXTS
and related documents

Contacting the WTO:

World Trade Organization
rue de Lausanne, 154
CH-1211 Geneva 21
Switzerland
www.wto.org

Information and External Relations Division
Tel. +41(0)22 739 5007 • Fax +41(0)22 739 5458 • Email: enquiries@wto.org

Publications Section
Tel. +41(0)22 739 5308 • Fax +41(0)22 739 5792 • Email: publications@wto.org

ISBN 978-92-870-3509-7

Contents

WORLD TRADE
ORGANIZATION

General Council 2004
General Council 31 July and
27 am

Doha Work Programme

Draft General Council Decision of 31 J

Ministerial Declaration

The Doha Round texts

and related documents

INTRODUCTION

This booklet replaces an earlier publication, *Doha Declarations*. It now includes the principal documents agreed by WTO member governments at important stages in the trade negotiations that were launched by the Doha Ministerial Conference in November 2001. The talks are nicknamed the Doha Round after the city where they were launched even though they mainly take place in Geneva. They are also called the Doha Development Agenda, partly to emphasize that development is a main objective, and partly to underscore that negotiations are one half of the work programme — the other half deals with problems that developing countries face in the implementation of the present agreements.

The negotiations proper are described as a "single undertaking". This means they form a single package of about 20 subjects, to be signed by each country with a single signature without any option to pick and choose between different subjects.

However, also reproduced here are some major decisions that follow on from the original Doha declarations, even though they are not part of the Doha Round and its "single undertaking".

Until the Doha Round concludes, this collection remains work in progress.

Before Doha   The compromise deal struck in the 1986–94 Uruguay Round included commitments to continue the reforms agreed in the round, in three subjects. The first to take effect was Article 23.4 of the Agreement on Trade Related Aspects of Intellectual Property Rights (TRIPS), which said members would negotiate creating a multilateral register for geographical indications for wines. Later spirits were added, and work began in 1997.

Of broader interest were negotiations in agriculture and services. These resumed in 2000, as agreed in Article 20 of the Agriculture Agreement and Article 19 of the General Agreement on Trade in Services. In 2001, members agreed guidelines and procedures for the services negotiations, considered an important step in the talks.

Meanwhile, in 2000, the General Council adopted a decision on a number of issues arising from the implementation of the WTO's present agreements.

Doha 2001   The 9–13 November 2001 Ministerial Conference in Doha, Qatar, was the fourth meeting of the WTO's topmost decision-making body. The declarations that WTO members adopted in Doha set up a work programme, the Doha Development Agenda, which includes trade negotiations (the Doha Round) and the issues arising from the implementation of the existing agreements.

In Doha, ministers also decided to postpone the deadline for some developing countries to eliminate export subsidies and for least-developed countries to provide protection for pharmaceutical patents and test data, and to tackle problems faced by countries unable to make generic versions of patented medicines. Detailed texts were needed to put these into practice. The one on subsidies was adopted by the Subsidies Committee during the Doha Ministerial Conference. Others came later.

The original aim was to reach agreement on almost all subjects in the negotiation by 1 January 2005. The only exceptions were the negotiation on improving and clarifying the Dispute Settlement Understanding (with a deadline of 31 May 2003 and technically not part of the "single undertaking") and the negotiations on a registration system for geographical indications for wines and spirits (with a deadline of the Fifth Ministerial Conference in 2003). Those deadlines were missed and the dates are now history.

The Doha Round after Doha   Because they are complex, the negotiations have progressed in stages, each stage narrowing down differences through interim agreements that represent the "acquis" — what has been acquired or achieved so far. The starting point was the Doha Declaration, which had set broad objectives for the round, reflecting the membership's divergent positions. The task of the negotiations was to find common ground and ultimately consensus.

Geneva 2003   The first major agreement in the Doha Round after the Doha Ministerial Conference was on special treatment in services for least-developed countries.

Geneva 2004   The General Council's decision of 1 August 2004 narrowed the gaps, focused the negotiations and raised them to a new level. This "July [2004] Package" decision included a number of annexes. Two of them are "Frameworks" for the negotiations in agriculture and non-agricultural market access, a term that is sometimes used for the entire package. (The 2004 decision sorted out disagreements that caused the 10–14 September 2003 Cancún Ministerial Conference to end in deadlock.)

Hong Kong 2005   The next major agreement was the declaration from the 13–18 December 2005 Hong Kong Ministerial Conference, which locked in a further narrowing of differences in the negotiations.

TRIPS and health   Meanwhile, in Doha but not part of the Doha Round, ministers included political statements, practical commitments and important clarifications in the main Doha Declaration and in a separate declaration on intellectual property and public health.

This led to decisions in 2002 to postpone (until 2016) the deadline for least-developed countries to protect pharmaceutical patents and test data, and in 2003 and 2005 on making it easier for countries to obtain cheaper generics produced elsewhere under compulsory licensing when they are unable to manufacture the medicines themselves.

And next?   The next step will be agreement on "modalities" — the way or method of doing something. In the Doha Development Agenda negotiations these are blueprints for the final deal, eg, how to cut tariffs, and reduce agricultural subsidies and support, along with flexibilities to deal with various sensitivities.

Once the modalities have been settled, countries will apply the formulas to tariffs on thousands of products and to a range of support programmes. Added to that will be pledges on how open their markets will be for services. The result will be the "schedules of commitments", which will take up tens of thousands of pages of the final deal. And also in the final deal will be new or revised agreements, the WTO's rule book.

Follow the talks here: *http://www.wto.org/dda*

Prologue

Before the Doha Ministerial Conference

- Mandate in Uruguay Round Agreements
- General Council decision on implementation
- Services guidelines and procedures

Marrakesh 1994. The entire Uruguay Round agreement at the signing ceremony: it included the seeds of what was to become the Doha Round.

Mandate in Uruguay Round Agreements

AGREEMENT ON AGRICULTURE, Article 20

Continuation of the Reform Process

Recognizing that the long-term objective of substantial progressive reductions in support and protection resulting in fundamental reform is an ongoing process, Members agree that negotiations for continuing the process will be initiated one year before the end of the implementation period, taking into account:

(a)   the experience to that date from implementing the reduction commitments;

(b)   the effects of the reduction commitments on world trade in agriculture;

(c)   non-trade concerns, special and differential treatment to developing country Members, and the objective to establish a fair and market-oriented agricultural trading system, and the other objectives and concerns mentioned in the preamble to this Agreement; and

(d)   what further commitments are necessary to achieve the above mentioned long-term objectives.

GENERAL AGREEMENT ON TRADE IN SERVICES, Article 19

Negotiation of Specific Commitments

1.   In pursuance of the objectives of this Agreement, Members shall enter into successive rounds of negotiations, beginning not later than five years from the date of entry into force of the WTO Agreement and periodically thereafter, with a view to achieving a progressively higher level of liberalization. Such negotiations shall be directed to the reduction or elimination of the adverse effects on trade in services of measures as a means of providing effective market access. This process shall take place with a view to promoting the interests of all participants on a mutually advantageous basis and to securing an overall balance of rights and obligations.

2.   The process of liberalization shall take place with due respect for national policy objectives and the level of development of individual Members, both overall and in individual sectors. There shall be appropriate flexibility for individual developing country Members for opening fewer sectors, liberalizing fewer types of transactions, progressively extending market access in line with their development situation and, when making access to their markets available to foreign service suppliers, attaching to such access conditions aimed at achieving the objectives referred to in Article IV.

3.   For each round, negotiating guidelines and procedures shall be established. For the purposes of establishing such guidelines, the Council for Trade in Services shall carry out an assessment of trade in services in overall terms and on a sectoral basis with reference to the objectives of this Agreement, including those set out in paragraph 1 of Article IV. Negotiating guidelines shall establish modalities for the treatment of liberalization undertaken autonomously by Members since previous negotiations, as well as for the special treatment for least-developed country Members under the provisions of paragraph 3 of Article IV.

4.   The process of progressive liberalization shall be advanced in each such round through bilateral, plurilateral or multilateral negotiations directed towards increasing the general level of specific commitments undertaken by Members under this Agreement.

TRIPS AGREEMENT, Article 23.4
Additional Protection for Geographical Indications for Wines and Spirits

4.   In order to facilitate the protection of geographical indications for wines, negotiations shall be undertaken in the Council for TRIPS concerning the establishment of a multilateral system of notification and registration of geographical indications for wines eligible for protection in those Members participating in the system.

General Council Decision
on Implementation Issues and Concerns

WT/L/384
19 December 2000
(00-5528)

GENERAL COUNCIL

Implementation-Related Issues and Concerns
Decision of 15 December 2000

The General Council,

Having regard to Articles IV.1, IV.2, IV.5 and IX.1 of the Marrakesh Agreement Establishing the World Trade Organization (WTO);

Considering the importance which Members attach to implementation-related issues and concerns as reflected in paragraphs 8 and 9 of the Geneva Ministerial Declaration, in the preparatory process for the third Ministerial Conference and in numerous subsequent discussions in the General Council;

Considering that the Decision of the General Council of 3 May 2000 provides that the General Council in Special Sessions shall address issues and concerns raised by Members in connection with the implementation of some WTO Agreements and Decisions;

Recalling further that the Decision of 3 May 2000 provides that the General Council shall assess the existing difficulties, identify ways needed to resolve them, and take decisions for appropriate action;

Taking into account the work programme on implementation issues agreed by the General Council at its first Special Session on 22 June 2000 which provides that, in the light of the progress made until then, the third Special Session will take decisions for appropriate action where possible;

Recalling the mandate given to the Chairman of the Council for Trade in Goods and the consultations held on the issue of transition periods under the Agreement on Trade-Related Investment Measures;

Taking into consideration the requests made to the Director-General to work with the relevant international standard-setting organizations and relevant intergovernmental organizations on the issue of the participation of developing countries in their work;

Recalling further that the following implementation-related issues were referred to the relevant WTO bodies at the Special Session held on 18 October 2000:

- in the area of Agriculture, the development of internationally agreed disciplines to govern the provision of export credits, export credit guarantees or insurance programmes pursuant to Article 10.2 of the Agreement on Agriculture, taking into account the provisions of paragraph 4 of the Decision on Measures Concerning the Possible Negative Effects of the Reform Programme on Least-Developed and Net Food-Importing Developing Countries;

- in the area of Sanitary and Phytosanitary measures, the concerns of developing countries regarding the equivalence of such measures;

- in the area of Technical Barriers to Trade, the problems faced by developing countries in both international standards and conformity assessment;

- in the area of Customs Valuation, the idea of information exchange between customs administrations on export values in doubtful cases, the addition of the cost of services in Article 8:1(b)(iv) and aspects of the residual method of determining customs value under Article 7 of the Customs Valuation Agreement; and,

- in the area of Trade-Related Aspects of Intellectual Property Rights (TRIPS), the issue of the relationship between the TRIPS Agreement and the Convention on Biological Diversity and the issue of the implementation of Article 66.2 of the Agreement on technology transfer.

Noting the reports on the above issues from the Chairpersons of the Council for Trade in Goods, the Council for Trade-Related Aspects of Intellectual Property Rights, and the Committees on Agriculture, Sanitary and Phytosanitary Measures, Technical Barriers to Trade and Customs Valuation, and from the Director-General;

Decides as follows:

1.   Agreement on Agriculture

1.1   Members shall ensure that their tariff rate quota regimes (TRQs) are administered in a transparent, equitable and non-discriminatory manner. In that context, they shall ensure that the notifications they provide to the Committee on Agriculture contain all the relevant information including details on guidelines and procedures on the allotment of TRQs. Members administering TRQs shall submit addenda to their notifications to the Committee on Agriculture (Table MA:1) by the time of the second regular meeting of the Committee in 2001.

1.2   The Committee on Agriculture shall examine possible means of improving the effectiveness of the implementation of the Decision on Measures Concerning the Possible Negative Effects of the Reform Programme on Least-Developed and Net Food-Importing Developing Countries and report to the General Council at the second regular meeting of the Council in 2001.

2.   **Agreement on the Application of Sanitary and Phytosanitary Measures**

In accordance with the request to the Director-General to work with the relevant international standard-setting organizations on the issue of the participation of developing countries in their work, these organizations are urged to ensure the participation of Members at different levels of development and from all geographic regions, throughout all phases of standard development.

3.   **Agreement on Technical Barriers to Trade**

In accordance with the request to the Director-General to work with the relevant international standard-setting organizations on the issue of the participation of developing countries in their work, these organizations are urged to ensure the participation of Members at different levels of development and from all geographic regions, throughout all phases of standard development.

4.   **Agreement on the Implementation of Article VII of the General Agreement on Tariffs and Trade 1994**

Noting that the process of examination and approval, in the Customs Valuation Committee, of individual requests from Members for extension of the five-year delay period in Article 20.1 is proceeding well, the General Council encourages the Committee to continue this work.

5.   **Agreement on Rules of Origin**

Members undertake to expedite the remaining work on the harmonization of non-preferential rules of origin, so as to complete it by the time of the

Fourth Ministerial Conference, or by the end of 2001 at the latest. The Chairman of the Committee on Rules of Origin shall report regularly, on his own responsibility, to the General Council on the progress being made. The first such report would be submitted to the Council at its first regular meeting in 2001, and subsequently at each regular meeting until the completion of the work programme.

6.   Agreement on Subsidies and Countervailing Measures

6.1   Taking into account the unique situation of Honduras as the only original Member of the WTO with a GNP per capita of less than US$ 1000 that was not included in Annex VII(b) to the Agreement on Subsidies and Countervailing Measures (SCM Agreement), Members call upon the Director-General to take appropriate steps, in accordance with WTO usual practice, to rectify the omission of Honduras from the list of Annex VII(b) countries.

6.2   The Committee on Subsidies and Countervailing Measures (SCM Committee) shall examine as an important part of its work all issues relating to Articles 27.5 and 27.6 of the SCM Agreement, including the possibility to establish export competitiveness on the basis of a period longer than two years.

6.3   The SCM Committee shall examine as an important part of its work the issues of aggregate and generalized rates of remission of import duties and of the definition of "inputs consumed in the production process", taking into account the particular needs of developing-country Members.

7.   Further Work

The General Council's Decision of 3 May 2000 on Implementation-Related Issues is reaffirmed. The General Council shall address the outstanding implementation-related issues and concerns, including those set out in paragraphs 21 and 22 of the revised Draft Ministerial Text dated 19 October 1999 (Job(99)/5868/Rev.1), as well as any other implementation-related issues raised by Members, as envisaged in the Decision of 3 May and the work programme agreed on 22 June 2000, with a view to completing the process no later than the Fourth Session of the Ministerial Conference.

Services Council Special Session Decision on Guidelines and Procedures for the Negotiations

S/L/93
29 March 2001
(01-1548)

Trade in Services

**GUIDELINES AND PROCEDURES FOR THE
NEGOTIATIONS ON TRADE IN SERVICES**
Adopted by the Special Session of the Council for
Trade in Services on 28 March 2001

I.   OBJECTIVES AND PRINCIPLES

1.   Pursuant to the objectives of the GATS, as stipulated in the Preamble and Article IV, and as required by Article XIX, the negotiations shall be conducted on the basis of progressive liberalisation as a means of promoting the economic growth of all trading partners and the development of developing countries, and recognizing the right of Members to regulate, and to introduce new regulations, on the supply of services. The negotiations shall aim to achieve progressively higher levels of liberalization of trade in services through the reduction or elimination of the adverse effects on trade in services of measures as a means of providing effective market access, and with a view to promoting the interests of all participants on a mutually advantageous basis and to securing an overall balance of rights and obligations.

2.   The negotiations shall aim to increase the participation of developing countries in trade in services. There shall be appropriate flexibility for individual developing country Members, as provided for by Article XIX:2. Special priority shall be granted to least-developed country Members as stipulated in Article IV:3.

3.   The process of liberalization shall take place with due respect for national policy objectives, the level of development and the size of economies of individual Members, both overall and in individual sectors. Due consideration should be given to the needs of small and medium-sized service suppliers, particularly those of developing countries.

4.   The negotiations shall take place within and shall respect the existing structure and principles of the GATS, including the right to specify sectors in which commitments will be undertaken and the four modes of supply.

II.   SCOPE

5.   There shall be no *a priori* exclusion of any service sector or mode of supply. Special attention shall be given to sectors and modes of supply of export interest to developing countries.

6.   MFN Exemptions shall be subject to negotiation according to paragraph 6 of the Annex on Article II (MFN) Exemptions. In such negotiations, appropriate flexibility shall be accorded to individual developing country Members.

7.   Negotiations on safeguards under Article X shall be completed by 15 March 2002 according to the Decision adopted by the Council for Trade in Services on 1 December 2000. Members shall aim to complete negotiations under Articles VI:4, XIII and XV prior to the conclusion of negotiations on specific commitments.

III.   MODALITIES AND PROCEDURES

8.   The negotiations shall be conducted in Special Sessions of the Council for Trade in Services, which will report on a regular basis to the General Council, in accordance with decisions taken by the General Council.

9.   Negotiations shall be transparent and open to all Members and acceding States and separate customs territories according to Decisions taken in this regard by the General Council.

10.   The starting point for the negotiation of specific commitments shall be the current schedules, without prejudice to the content of requests.

11.   Liberalization shall be advanced through bilateral, plurilateral or multilateral negotiations. The main method of negotiation shall be the request-offer approach.

12.   There shall be appropriate flexibility for individual developing country Members for opening fewer sectors, liberalizing fewer types of transactions, progressively extending market access in line with their development situation and, when making access to their markets available to foreign service suppliers, attaching to such access conditions aimed at achieving the objectives referred to in Article IV.

13.   Based on multilaterally agreed criteria, account shall be taken and credit shall be given in the negotiations for autonomous liberalization undertaken by Members since previous negotiations. Members shall endeavour to develop such criteria prior to the start of negotiation of specific commitments.

14.   The Council for Trade in Services in Special Sessions shall continue to carry out an assessment of trade in services in overall terms and on a sectoral basis with reference to the objectives of the GATS and of Article IV in particular. This shall be an ongoing activity of the Council and negotiations shall be adjusted in the light of the results of the assessment. In accordance with Article XXV of the GATS, technical assistance shall be provided to developing country Members, on request, in order to carry out national/regional assessments.

15.   To ensure the effective implementation of Articles IV and XIX:2, the Council for Trade in Services in Special Session, when reviewing progress in negotiations, shall consider the extent to which Article IV is being implemented and suggest ways and means of promoting the goals established therein. In implementing Article IV consideration shall also be given to the needs of small service suppliers of developing countries. It shall also conduct an evaluation, before the completion of the negotiations, of the results attained in terms of the objectives of Article IV.

16.   While the Council for Trade in Services in Special Sessions may establish subsidiary bodies as it deems necessary, the proliferation of such bodies should be avoided to the maximum extent possible. Existing subsidiary bodies shall be utilised to their maximum capacity.

17.   The needs of smaller delegations should be taken into account, e.g. by scheduling meetings in sequence and not in parallel.

18.   The Council for Trade in Services in Special Sessions shall, when appropriate, develop time schedules for the conduct of the negotiations in accordance with any relevant decisions taken by the General Council.

Doha Ministerial Conference

14 November 2001

- Doha Declaration
- Declaration on TRIPS and Public Health
- Doha Implementation Decision
- Doha EU-ACP Waiver
- Doha Banana Decision
- Doha Subsidies Procedure

Doha 2001: Where the Doha Round was launched.

The Doha
Ministerial Declaration

WT/MIN(01)/DEC/1
20 November 2001
(01-5859)

MINISTERIAL CONFERENCE
Fourth Session
Doha, 9–14 November 2001

MINISTERIAL DECLARATION
Adopted on 14 November 2001

1.   The multilateral trading system embodied in the World Trade Organization has contributed significantly to economic growth, development and employment throughout the past fifty years. We are determined, particularly in the light of the global economic slowdown, to maintain the process of reform and liberalization of trade policies, thus ensuring that the system plays its full part in promoting recovery, growth and development. We therefore strongly reaffirm the principles and objectives set out in the Marrakesh Agreement Establishing the World Trade Organization, and pledge to reject the use of protectionism.

2.   International trade can play a major role in the promotion of economic development and the alleviation of poverty. We recognize the need for all our peoples to benefit from the increased opportunities and welfare gains that the multilateral trading system generates. The majority of WTO Members are developing countries. We seek to place their needs and interests at the heart of the Work Programme adopted in this Declaration. Recalling the Preamble to the Marrakesh Agreement, we shall continue to make positive efforts designed to ensure that developing countries, and especially the least-developed among them, secure a share in the growth of world trade commensurate with the needs of their economic development. In this context, enhanced market access, balanced rules, and well targeted, sustainably financed technical assistance and capacity-building programmes have important roles to play.

3.   We recognize the particular vulnerability of the least-developed countries and the special structural difficulties they face in the global economy. We are committed to addressing the marginalization of least-developed countries in international trade and to improving their effective participation in the multilateral trading system. We recall the commitments made by Ministers at our meetings in Marrakesh, Singapore and Geneva, and by the international community at the Third UN Conference on Least-Developed Countries in Brussels, to help

least-developed countries secure beneficial and meaningful integration into the multilateral trading system and the global economy. We are determined that the WTO will play its part in building effectively on these commitments under the Work Programme we are establishing.

4.   We stress our commitment to the WTO as the unique forum for global trade rule-making and liberalization, while also recognizing that regional trade agreements can play an important role in promoting the liberalization and expansion of trade and in fostering development.

5.   We are aware that the challenges Members face in a rapidly changing international environment cannot be addressed through measures taken in the trade field alone. We shall continue to work with the Bretton Woods institutions for greater coherence in global economic policy-making.

6.   We strongly reaffirm our commitment to the objective of sustainable development, as stated in the Preamble to the Marrakesh Agreement. We are convinced that the aims of upholding and safeguarding an open and non-discriminatory multilateral trading system, and acting for the protection of the environment and the promotion of sustainable development can and must be mutually supportive. We take note of the efforts by Members to conduct national environmental assessments of trade policies on a voluntary basis. We recognize that under WTO rules no country should be prevented from taking measures for the protection of human, animal or plant life or health, or of the environment at the levels it considers appropriate, subject to the requirement that they are not applied in a manner which would constitute a means of arbitrary or unjustifiable discrimination between countries where the same conditions prevail, or a disguised restriction on international trade, and are otherwise in accordance with the provisions of the WTO Agreements. We welcome the WTO's continued cooperation with UNEP and other inter-governmental environmental organizations. We encourage efforts to promote cooperation between the WTO and relevant international environmental and developmental organizations, especially in the lead-up to the World Summit on Sustainable Development to be held in Johannesburg, South Africa, in September 2002.

7.   We reaffirm the right of Members under the General Agreement on Trade in Services to regulate, and to introduce new regulations on, the supply of services.

8.   We reaffirm our declaration made at the Singapore Ministerial Conference regarding internationally recognized core labour standards. We take note of work under way in the International Labour Organization (ILO) on the social dimension of globalization.

9.   We note with particular satisfaction that this Conference has completed the WTO accession procedures for China and Chinese Taipei. We also welcome the accession as new Members, since our last Session, of Albania, Croatia, Georgia, Jordan, Lithuania, Moldova and Oman, and note the extensive market-access commitments already made by these countries on accession. These accessions will greatly strengthen the multilateral trading system, as will those of the 28 countries now negotiating their accession. We therefore attach great importance to concluding accession proceedings as quickly as possible. In particular, we are committed to accelerating the accession of least-developed countries.

10.   Recognizing the challenges posed by an expanding WTO membership, we confirm our collective responsibility to ensure internal transparency and the effective participation of all Members. While emphasizing the intergovernmental character of the organization, we are committed to making the WTO's operations more transparent, including through more effective and prompt dissemination of information, and to improve dialogue with the public. We shall therefore at the national and multilateral levels continue to promote a better public understanding of the WTO and to communicate the benefits of a liberal, rules-based multilateral trading system.

11.   In view of these considerations, we hereby agree to undertake the broad and balanced Work Programme set out below. This incorporates both an expanded negotiating agenda and other important decisions and activities necessary to address the challenges facing the multilateral trading system.

WORK PROGRAMME

IMPLEMENTATION-RELATED ISSUES AND CONCERNS

12.   We attach the utmost importance to the implementation-related issues and concerns raised by Members and are determined to find appropriate solutions to them. In this connection, and having regard to the General Council Decisions of 3 May and 15 December 2000, we further adopt the Decision on Implementation-Related Issues and Concerns in document WT/MIN(01)/17 to address a number of implementation problems faced by Members. We agree that negotiations on outstanding implementation issues shall be an integral part of the Work Programme we are establishing, and that agreements reached at an early stage in these negotiations shall be treated in accordance with the provisions of paragraph 47 below. In this regard, we shall proceed as follows: (a) where we provide a specific negotiating mandate in this Declaration, the relevant implementation issues shall be addressed under that mandate; (b) the other outstanding implementation issues shall be

addressed as a matter of priority by the relevant WTO bodies, which shall report to the Trade Negotiations Committee, established under paragraph 46 below, by the end of 2002 for appropriate action.

AGRICULTURE

13.   We recognize the work already undertaken in the negotiations initiated in early 2000 under Article 20 of the Agreement on Agriculture, including the large number of negotiating proposals submitted on behalf of a total of 121 Members. We recall the long-term objective referred to in the Agreement to establish a fair and market-oriented trading system through a programme of fundamental reform encompassing strengthened rules and specific commitments on support and protection in order to correct and prevent restrictions and distortions in world agricultural markets. We reconfirm our commitment to this programme. Building on the work carried out to date and without prejudging the outcome of the negotiations we commit ourselves to comprehensive negotiations aimed at: substantial improvements in market access; reductions of, with a view to phasing out, all forms of export subsidies; and substantial reductions in trade-distorting domestic support. We agree that special and differential treatment for developing countries shall be an integral part of all elements of the negotiations and shall be embodied in the Schedules of concessions and commitments and as appropriate in the rules and disciplines to be negotiated, so as to be operationally effective and to enable developing countries to effectively take account of their development needs, including food security and rural development. We take note of the non-trade concerns reflected in the negotiating proposals submitted by Members and confirm that non-trade concerns will be taken into account in the negotiations as provided for in the Agreement on Agriculture.

14.   Modalities for the further commitments, including provisions for special and differential treatment, shall be established no later than 31 March 2003. Participants shall submit their comprehensive draft Schedules based on these modalities no later than the date of the Fifth Session of the Ministerial Conference. The negotiations, including with respect to rules and disciplines and related legal texts, shall be concluded as part and at the date of conclusion of the negotiating agenda as a whole.

SERVICES

15.   The negotiations on trade in services shall be conducted with a view to promoting the economic growth of all trading partners and the development of developing and least-developed countries. We recognize the work already undertaken in the negotiations, initiated

in January 2000 under Article XIX of the General Agreement on Trade in Services, and the large number of proposals submitted by Members on a wide range of sectors and several horizontal issues, as well as on movement of natural persons. We reaffirm the Guidelines and Procedures for the Negotiations adopted by the Council for Trade in Services on 28 March 2001 as the basis for continuing the negotiations, with a view to achieving the objectives of the General Agreement on Trade in Services, as stipulated in the Preamble, Article IV and Article XIX of that Agreement. Participants shall submit initial requests for specific commitments by 30 June 2002 and initial offers by 31 March 2003.

MARKET ACCESS FOR NON-AGRICULTURAL PRODUCTS

16.   We agree to negotiations which shall aim, by modalities to be agreed, to reduce or as appropriate eliminate tariffs, including the reduction or elimination of tariff peaks, high tariffs, and tariff escalation, as well as non-tariff barriers, in particular on products of export interest to developing countries. Product coverage shall be comprehensive and without *a priori* exclusions. The negotiations shall take fully into account the special needs and interests of developing and least-developed country participants, including through less than full reciprocity in reduction commitments, in accordance with the relevant provisions of Article XXVIII *bis* of GATT 1994 and the provisions cited in paragraph 50 below. To this end, the modalities to be agreed will include appropriate studies and capacity-building measures to assist least-developed countries to participate effectively in the negotiations.

TRADE-RELATED ASPECTS OF INTELLECTUAL PROPERTY RIGHTS

17.   We stress the importance we attach to implementation and interpretation of the Agreement on Trade-Related Aspects of Intellectual Property Rights (TRIPS Agreement) in a manner supportive of public health, by promoting both access to existing medicines and research and development into new medicines and, in this connection, are adopting a separate Declaration.

18.   With a view to completing the work started in the Council for Trade-Related Aspects of Intellectual Property Rights (Council for TRIPS) on the implementation of Article 23.4, we agree to negotiate the establishment of a multilateral system of notification and registration of geographical indications for wines and spirits by the Fifth Session of the Ministerial Conference. We note that issues related to the extension of the protection of geographical indications provided for in Article 23 to products other than wines and spirits will be addressed in the Council for TRIPS pursuant to paragraph 12 of this Declaration.

19.   We instruct the Council for TRIPS, in pursuing its work programme including under the review of Article 27.3(b), the review of the implementation of the TRIPS Agreement under Article 71.1 and the work foreseen pursuant to paragraph 12 of this Declaration, to examine, *inter alia*, the relationship between the TRIPS Agreement and the Convention on Biological Diversity, the protection of traditional knowledge and folklore, and other relevant new developments raised by Members pursuant to Article 71.1. In undertaking this work, the TRIPS Council shall be guided by the objectives and principles set out in Articles 7 and 8 of the TRIPS Agreement and shall take fully into account the development dimension.

RELATIONSHIP BETWEEN TRADE AND INVESTMENT

20.   Recognizing the case for a multilateral framework to secure transparent, stable and predictable conditions for long-term cross-border investment, particularly foreign direct investment, that will contribute to the expansion of trade, and the need for enhanced technical assistance and capacity-building in this area as referred to in paragraph 21, we agree that negotiations will take place after the Fifth Session of the Ministerial Conference on the basis of a decision to be taken, by explicit consensus, at that Session on modalities of negotiations.

21.   We recognize the needs of developing and least-developed countries for enhanced support for technical assistance and capacity building in this area, including policy analysis and development so that they may better evaluate the implications of closer multilateral cooperation for their development policies and objectives, and human and institutional development. To this end, we shall work in cooperation with other relevant intergovernmental organisations, including UNCTAD, and through appropriate regional and bilateral channels, to provide strengthened and adequately resourced assistance to respond to these needs.

22.   In the period until the Fifth Session, further work in the Working Group on the Relationship Between Trade and Investment will focus on the clarification of: scope and definition; transparency; non-discrimination; modalities for pre-establishment commitments based on a GATS-type, positive list approach; development provisions; exceptions and balance-of-payments safeguards; consultation and the settlement of disputes between Members. Any framework should reflect in a balanced manner the interests of home and host countries, and take due account of the development policies and objectives of host governments as well as their right to regulate in the public interest. The special development, trade and financial needs of developing and least-developed countries should be taken into account as an integral part of any framework, which should enable Members to undertake obligations and commitments commensurate with their individual needs and circumstances.

Due regard should be paid to other relevant WTO provisions. Account should be taken, as appropriate, of existing bilateral and regional arrangements on investment.

INTERACTION BETWEEN TRADE AND COMPETITION POLICY

23.   Recognizing the case for a multilateral framework to enhance the contribution of competition policy to international trade and development, and the need for enhanced technical assistance and capacity-building in this area as referred to in paragraph 24, we agree that negotiations will take place after the Fifth Session of the Ministerial Conference on the basis of a decision to be taken, by explicit consensus, at that Session on modalities of negotiations.

24.   We recognize the needs of developing and least-developed countries for enhanced support for technical assistance and capacity building in this area, including policy analysis and development so that they may better evaluate the implications of closer multilateral cooperation for their development policies and objectives, and human and institutional development. To this end, we shall work in cooperation with other relevant intergovernmental organisations, including UNCTAD, and through appropriate regional and bilateral channels, to provide strengthened and adequately resourced assistance to respond to these needs.

25.   In the period until the Fifth Session, further work in the Working Group on the Interaction between Trade and Competition Policy will focus on the clarification of: core principles, including transparency, non-discrimination and procedural fairness, and provisions on hardcore cartels; modalities for voluntary cooperation; and support for progressive reinforcement of competition institutions in developing countries through capacity building. Full account shall be taken of the needs of developing and least-developed country participants and appropriate flexibility provided to address them.

TRANSPARENCY IN GOVERNMENT PROCUREMENT

26.   Recognizing the case for a multilateral agreement on transparency in government procurement and the need for enhanced technical assistance and capacity building in this area, we agree that negotiations will take place after the Fifth Session of the Ministerial Conference on the basis of a decision to be taken, by explicit consensus, at that Session on modalities of negotiations. These negotiations will build on the progress made in the Working Group on Transparency in Government Procurement by that time and take into account participants' development priorities, especially those of least-developed country participants. Negotiations shall be limited to the transparency aspects and therefore will not restrict the scope for countries to give preferences to domestic supplies and suppliers. We commit

ourselves to ensuring adequate technical assistance and support for capacity building both during the negotiations and after their conclusion.

TRADE FACILITATION

27.   Recognizing the case for further expediting the movement, release and clearance of goods, including goods in transit, and the need for enhanced technical assistance and capacity building in this area, we agree that negotiations will take place after the Fifth Session of the Ministerial Conference on the basis of a decision to be taken, by explicit consensus, at that Session on modalities of negotiations. In the period until the Fifth Session, the Council for Trade in Goods shall review and as appropriate, clarify and improve relevant aspects of Articles V, VIII and X of the GATT 1994 and identify the trade facilitation needs and priorities of Members, in particular developing and least-developed countries. We commit ourselves to ensuring adequate technical assistance and support for capacity building in this area.

WTO RULES

28.   In the light of experience and of the increasing application of these instruments by Members, we agree to negotiations aimed at clarifying and improving disciplines under the Agreements on Implementation of Article VI of the GATT 1994 and on Subsidies and Countervailing Measures, while preserving the basic concepts, principles and effectiveness of these Agreements and their instruments and objectives, and taking into account the needs of developing and least-developed participants. In the initial phase of the negotiations, participants will indicate the provisions, including disciplines on trade distorting practices, that they seek to clarify and improve in the subsequent phase. In the context of these negotiations, participants shall also aim to clarify and improve WTO disciplines on fisheries subsidies, taking into account the importance of this sector to developing countries. We note that fisheries subsidies are also referred to in paragraph 31.

29.   We also agree to negotiations aimed at clarifying and improving disciplines and procedures under the existing WTO provisions applying to regional trade agreements. The negotiations shall take into account the developmental aspects of regional trade agreements.

DISPUTE SETTLEMENT UNDERSTANDING

30.   We agree to negotiations on improvements and clarifications of the Dispute Settlement Understanding. The negotiations should be based on the work done thus far as well as any additional proposals by Members, and aim to agree on improvements and

clarifications not later than May 2003, at which time we will take steps to ensure that the results enter into force as soon as possible thereafter.

TRADE AND ENVIRONMENT

31.   With a view to enhancing the mutual supportiveness of trade and environment, we agree to negotiations, without prejudging their outcome, on:

(i)   the relationship between existing WTO rules and specific trade obligations set out in multilateral environmental agreements (MEAs). The negotiations shall be limited in scope to the applicability of such existing WTO rules as among parties to the MEA in question. The negotiations shall not prejudice the WTO rights of any Member that is not a party to the MEA in question;

(ii)   procedures for regular information exchange between MEA Secretariats and the relevant WTO committees, and the criteria for the granting of observer status;

(iii)   the reduction or, as appropriate, elimination of tariff and non-tariff barriers to environmental goods and services.

We note that fisheries subsidies form part of the negotiations provided for in paragraph 28.

32.   We instruct the Committee on Trade and Environment, in pursuing work on all items on its agenda within its current terms of reference, to give particular attention to:

(i)   the effect of environmental measures on market access, especially in relation to developing countries, in particular the least-developed among them, and those situations in which the elimination or reduction of trade restrictions and distortions would benefit trade, the environment and development;

(ii)   the relevant provisions of the Agreement on Trade-Related Aspects of Intellectual Property Rights; and

(iii)   labelling requirements for environmental purposes.

Work on these issues should include the identification of any need to clarify relevant WTO rules. The Committee shall report to the Fifth Session of the Ministerial Conference, and make recommendations, where appropriate, with respect to future action, including the desirability of negotiations. The outcome of this work as well as the negotiations carried out under paragraph 31(i) and (ii) shall be compatible with the open and non-discriminatory nature of the multilateral trading system, shall not add to or diminish the rights and obligations of Members under existing WTO agreements, in particular the Agreement on the Application of Sanitary and Phytosanitary Measures, nor alter the balance of these rights and obligations, and will take into account the needs of developing and least-developed countries.

33.   We recognize the importance of technical assistance and capacity building in the field of trade and environment to developing countries, in particular the least-developed among them. We also encourage that expertise and experience be shared with Members wishing to perform environmental reviews at the national level. A report shall be prepared on these activities for the Fifth Session.

ELECTRONIC COMMERCE

34.   We take note of the work which has been done in the General Council and other relevant bodies since the Ministerial Declaration of 20 May 1998 and agree to continue the Work Programme on Electronic Commerce. The work to date demonstrates that electronic commerce creates new challenges and opportunities for trade for Members at all stages of development, and we recognize the importance of creating and maintaining an environment which is favourable to the future development of electronic commerce. We instruct the General Council to consider the most appropriate institutional arrangements for handling the Work Programme, and to report on further progress to the Fifth Session of the Ministerial Conference. We declare that Members will maintain their current practice of not imposing customs duties on electronic transmissions until the Fifth Session.

SMALL ECONOMIES

35.   We agree to a work programme, under the auspices of the General Council, to examine issues relating to the trade of small economies. The objective of this work is to frame responses to the trade-related issues identified for the fuller integration of small, vulnerable economies into the multilateral trading system, and not to create a sub-category of WTO Members. The General Council shall review the work programme and make recommendations for action to the Fifth Session of the Ministerial Conference.

TRADE, DEBT AND FINANCE

36.   We agree to an examination, in a Working Group under the auspices of the General Council, of the relationship between trade, debt and finance, and of any possible recommendations on steps that might be taken within the mandate and competence of the WTO to enhance the capacity of the multilateral trading system to contribute to a durable

solution to the problem of external indebtedness of developing and least-developed countries, and to strengthen the coherence of international trade and financial policies, with a view to safeguarding the multilateral trading system from the effects of financial and monetary instability. The General Council shall report to the Fifth Session of the Ministerial Conference on progress in the examination.

TRADE AND TRANSFER OF TECHNOLOGY

37. We agree to an examination, in a Working Group under the auspices of the General Council, of the relationship between trade and transfer of technology, and of any possible recommendations on steps that might be taken within the mandate of the WTO to increase flows of technology to developing countries. The General Council shall report to the Fifth Session of the Ministerial Conference on progress in the examination.

TECHNICAL COOPERATION AND CAPACITY BUILDING

38. We confirm that technical cooperation and capacity building are core elements of the development dimension of the multilateral trading system, and we welcome and endorse the New Strategy for WTO Technical Cooperation for Capacity Building, Growth and Integration. We instruct the Secretariat, in coordination with other relevant agencies, to support domestic efforts for mainstreaming trade into national plans for economic development and strategies for poverty reduction. The delivery of WTO technical assistance shall be designed to assist developing and least-developed countries and low-income countries in transition to adjust to WTO rules and disciplines, implement obligations and exercise the rights of membership, including drawing on the benefits of an open, rules-based multilateral trading system. Priority shall also be accorded to small, vulnerable, and transition economies, as well as to Members and Observers without representation in Geneva. We reaffirm our support for the valuable work of the International Trade Centre, which should be enhanced.

39. We underscore the urgent necessity for the effective coordinated delivery of technical assistance with bilateral donors, in the OECD Development Assistance Committee and relevant international and regional intergovernmental institutions, within a coherent policy framework and timetable. In the coordinated delivery of technical assistance, we instruct the Director-General to consult with the relevant agencies, bilateral donors and beneficiaries, to identify ways of enhancing and rationalizing the Integrated Framework for Trade-Related Technical Assistance to Least-Developed Countries and the Joint Integrated Technical Assistance Programme (JITAP).

40.   We agree that there is a need for technical assistance to benefit from secure and predictable funding. We therefore instruct the Committee on Budget, Finance and Administration to develop a plan for adoption by the General Council in December 2001 that will ensure long-term funding for WTO technical assistance at an overall level no lower than that of the current year and commensurate with the activities outlined above.

41.   We have established firm commitments on technical cooperation and capacity building in various paragraphs in this Ministerial Declaration. We reaffirm these specific commitments contained in paragraphs 16, 21, 24, 26, 27, 33, 38-40, 42 and 43, and also reaffirm the understanding in paragraph 2 on the important role of sustainably financed technical assistance and capacity-building programmes. We instruct the Director-General to report to the Fifth Session of the Ministerial Conference, with an interim report to the General Council in December 2002 on the implementation and adequacy of these commitments in the identified paragraphs.

LEAST-DEVELOPED COUNTRIES

42.   We acknowledge the seriousness of the concerns expressed by the least-developed countries (LDCs) in the Zanzibar Declaration adopted by their Ministers in July 2001. We recognize that the integration of the LDCs into the multilateral trading system requires meaningful market access, support for the diversification of their production and export base, and trade-related technical assistance and capacity building. We agree that the meaningful integration of LDCs into the trading system and the global economy will involve efforts by all WTO Members. We commit ourselves to the objective of duty-free, quota-free market access for products originating from LDCs. In this regard, we welcome the significant market access improvements by WTO Members in advance of the Third UN Conference on LDCs (LDC-III), in Brussels, May 2001. We further commit ourselves to consider additional measures for progressive improvements in market access for LDCs. Accession of LDCs remains a priority for the Membership. We agree to work to facilitate and accelerate negotiations with acceding LDCs. We instruct the Secretariat to reflect the priority we attach to LDCs' accessions in the annual plans for technical assistance. We reaffirm the commitments we undertook at LDC-III, and agree that the WTO should take into account, in designing its work programme for LDCs, the trade-related elements of the Brussels Declaration and Programme of Action, consistent with the WTO's mandate, adopted at LDC-III. We instruct the Sub-Committee for Least-Developed Countries to design such a work programme and to report on the agreed work programme to the General Council at its first meeting in 2002.

43.   We endorse the Integrated Framework for Trade-Related Technical Assistance to Least-Developed Countries (IF) as a viable model for LDCs' trade development. We urge development partners to significantly increase contributions to the IF Trust Fund and WTO extra-budgetary trust funds in favour of LDCs. We urge the core agencies, in coordination with development partners, to explore the enhancement of the IF with a view to addressing the supply-side constraints of LDCs and the extension of the model to all LDCs, following the review of the IF and the appraisal of the ongoing Pilot Scheme in selected LDCs. We request the Director-General, following coordination with heads of the other agencies, to provide an interim report to the General Council in December 2002 and a full report to the Fifth Session of the Ministerial Conference on all issues affecting LDCs.

SPECIAL AND DIFFERENTIAL TREATMENT

44.   We reaffirm that provisions for special and differential treatment are an integral part of the WTO Agreements. We note the concerns expressed regarding their operation in addressing specific constraints faced by developing countries, particularly least-developed countries. In that connection, we also note that some Members have proposed a Framework Agreement on Special and Differential Treatment (WT/GC/W/442). We therefore agree that all special and differential treatment provisions shall be reviewed with a view to strengthening them and making them more precise, effective and operational. In this connection, we endorse the work programme on special and differential treatment set out in the Decision on Implementation-Related Issues and Concerns.

ORGANIZATION AND MANAGEMENT OF THE WORK PROGRAMME

45.   The negotiations to be pursued under the terms of this Declaration shall be concluded not later than 1 January 2005. The Fifth Session of the Ministerial Conference will take stock of progress in the negotiations, provide any necessary political guidance, and take decisions as necessary. When the results of the negotiations in all areas have been established, a Special Session of the Ministerial Conference will be held to take decisions regarding the adoption and implementation of those results.

46.   The overall conduct of the negotiations shall be supervised by a Trade Negotiations Committee under the authority of the General Council. The Trade Negotiations Committee shall hold its first meeting not later than 31 January 2002. It shall establish appropriate negotiating mechanisms as required and supervise the progress of the negotiations.

47.   With the exception of the improvements and clarifications of the Dispute Settlement Understanding, the conduct, conclusion and entry into force of the outcome of the

negotiations shall be treated as parts of a single undertaking. However, agreements reached at an early stage may be implemented on a provisional or a definitive basis. Early agreements shall be taken into account in assessing the overall balance of the negotiations.

48.   Negotiations shall be open to:

(i)   all Members of the WTO; and

(ii)   States and separate customs territories currently in the process of accession and those that inform Members, at a regular meeting of the General Council, of their intention to negotiate the terms of their membership and for whom an accession working party is established.

Decisions on the outcomes of the negotiations shall be taken only by WTO Members.

49.   The negotiations shall be conducted in a transparent manner among participants, in order to facilitate the effective participation of all. They shall be conducted with a view to ensuring benefits to all participants and to achieving an overall balance in the outcome of the negotiations.

50.   The negotiations and the other aspects of the Work Programme shall take fully into account the principle of special and differential treatment for developing and least-developed countries embodied in: Part IV of the GATT 1994; the Decision of 28 November 1979 on Differential and More Favourable Treatment, Reciprocity and Fuller Participation of Developing Countries; the Uruguay Round Decision on Measures in Favour of Least-Developed Countries; and all other relevant WTO provisions.

51.   The Committee on Trade and Development and the Committee on Trade and Environment shall, within their respective mandates, each act as a forum to identify and debate developmental and environmental aspects of the negotiations, in order to help achieve the objective of having sustainable development appropriately reflected.

52.   Those elements of the Work Programme which do not involve negotiations are also accorded a high priority. They shall be pursued under the overall supervision of the General Council, which shall report on progress to the Fifth Session of the Ministerial Conference.

Ministerial Declaration on the TRIPS Agreement and Public Health

WT/MIN(01)/DEC/2
20 November 2001
(01-5860)

MINISTERIAL CONFERENCE
Fourth Session
Doha, 9–14 November 2001

DECLARATION ON THE TRIPS AGREEMENT
AND PUBLIC HEALTH
Adopted on 14 November 2001

1.   We recognize the gravity of the public health problems afflicting many developing and least-developed countries, especially those resulting from HIV/AIDS, tuberculosis, malaria and other epidemics.

2.   We stress the need for the WTO Agreement on Trade-Related Aspects of Intellectual Property Rights (TRIPS Agreement) to be part of the wider national and international action to address these problems.

3.   We recognize that intellectual property protection is important for the development of new medicines. We also recognize the concerns about its effects on prices.

4.   We agree that the TRIPS Agreement does not and should not prevent Members from taking measures to protect public health. Accordingly, while reiterating our commitment to the TRIPS Agreement, we affirm that the Agreement can and should be interpreted and implemented in a manner supportive of WTO Members' right to protect public health and, in particular, to promote access to medicines for all.

In this connection, we reaffirm the right of WTO Members to use, to the full, the provisions in the TRIPS Agreement, which provide flexibility for this purpose.

5.   Accordingly and in the light of paragraph 4 above, while maintaining our commitments in the TRIPS Agreement, we recognize that these flexibilities include:

(a)   In applying the customary rules of interpretation of public international law, each provision of the TRIPS Agreement shall be read in the light of the object and purpose of the Agreement as expressed, in particular, in its objectives and principles.

(b)   Each Member has the right to grant compulsory licences and the freedom to determine the grounds upon which such licences are granted.

(c)   Each Member has the right to determine what constitutes a national emergency or other circumstances of extreme urgency, it being understood that public health crises, including those relating to HIV/AIDS, tuberculosis, malaria and other epidemics, can represent a national emergency or other circumstances of extreme urgency.

(d)   The effect of the provisions in the TRIPS Agreement that are relevant to the exhaustion of intellectual property rights is to leave each Member free to establish its own regime for such exhaustion without challenge, subject to the MFN and national treatment provisions of Articles 3 and 4.

6.   We recognize that WTO Members with insufficient or no manufacturing capacities in the pharmaceutical sector could face difficulties in making effective use of compulsory licensing under the TRIPS Agreement. We instruct the Council for TRIPS to find an expeditious solution to this problem and to report to the General Council before the end of 2002.

7.   We reaffirm the commitment of developed-country Members to provide incentives to their enterprises and institutions to promote and encourage technology transfer to least-developed country Members pursuant to Article 66.2. We also agree that the least-developed country Members will not be obliged, with respect to pharmaceutical products, to implement or apply Sections 5 and 7 of Part II of the TRIPS Agreement or to enforce rights provided for under these Sections until 1 January 2016, without prejudice to the right of least-developed country Members to seek other extensions of the transition periods as provided for in Article 66.1 of the TRIPS Agreement. We instruct the Council for TRIPS to take the necessary action to give effect to this pursuant to Article 66.1 of the TRIPS Agreement.

Ministerial Decision on Implementation-Related Issues and Concerns

WT/MIN(01)/17

20 November 2001

(01-5858)

MINISTERIAL CONFERENCE
Fourth Session
Doha, 9–14 November 2001

IMPLEMENTATION-RELATED ISSUES AND CONCERNS
Decision of 14 November 2001

The Ministerial Conference,

Having regard to Articles IV.1, IV.5 and IX of the Marrakesh Agreement Establishing the World Trade Organization (WTO);

Mindful of the importance that Members attach to the increased participation of developing countries in the multilateral trading system, and of the need to ensure that the system responds fully to the needs and interests of all participants;

Determined to take concrete action to address issues and concerns that have been raised by many developing-country Members regarding the implementation of some WTO Agreements and Decisions, including the difficulties and resource constraints that have been encountered in the implementation of obligations in various areas;

Recalling the 3 May 2000 Decision of the General Council to meet in special sessions to address outstanding implementation issues, and to assess the existing difficulties, identify ways needed to resolve them, and take decisions for appropriate action not later than the Fourth Session of the Ministerial Conference;

Noting the actions taken by the General Council in pursuance of this mandate at its Special Sessions in October and December 2000 (WT/L/384), as well as the review and further discussion undertaken at the Special Sessions held in April, July and October 2001, including the referral of additional issues to relevant WTO bodies or their chairpersons for further work;

Noting also the reports on the issues referred to the General Council from subsidiary bodies and their chairpersons and from the Director-General, and the discussions as well as the clarifications provided and understandings reached on implementation issues in the intensive informal and formal meetings held under this process since May 2000;

Decides as follows:

1.   General Agreement on Tariffs and Trade 1994 (GATT 1994)

    1.1   Reaffirms that Article XVIII of the GATT 1994 is a special and differential treatment provision for developing countries and that recourse to it should be less onerous than to Article XII of the GATT 1994.

    1.2   Noting the issues raised in the report of the Chairperson of the Committee on Market Access (WT/GC/50) concerning the meaning to be given to the phrase "substantial interest" in paragraph 2(d) of Article XIII of the GATT 1994, the Market Access Committee is directed to give further consideration to the issue and make recommendations to the General Council as expeditiously as possible but in any event not later than the end of 2002.

2.   Agreement on Agriculture

    2.1   Urges Members to exercise restraint in challenging measures notified under the green box by developing countries to promote rural development and adequately address food security concerns.

    2.2   Takes note of the report of the Committee on Agriculture (G/AG/11) regarding the implementation of the Decision on Measures Concerning the Possible Negative Effects of the Reform Programme on Least-Developed and Net Food-Importing Developing Countries, and approves the recommendations contained therein regarding (i) food aid; (ii) technical and financial assistance in the context of aid programmes to improve agricultural productivity and infrastructure; (iii) financing normal levels of commercial imports of basic foodstuffs; and (iv) review of follow-up.

    2.3   Takes note of the report of the Committee on Agriculture (G/AG/11) regarding the implementation of Article 10.2 of the Agreement on Agriculture, and approves the recommendations and reporting requirements contained therein.

    2.4   Takes note of the report of the Committee on Agriculture (G/AG/11) regarding the administration of tariff rate quotas and the submission by Members of addenda to their notifications, and endorses the decision by the Committee to keep this matter under review.

3. Agreement on the Application of Sanitary and Phytosanitary Measures

3.1   Where the appropriate level of sanitary and phytosanitary protection allows scope for the phased introduction of new sanitary and phytosanitary measures, the phrase "longer time-frame for compliance" referred to in Article 10.2 of the Agreement on the Application of Sanitary and Phytosanitary Measures, shall be understood to mean normally a period of not less than 6 months. Where the appropriate level of sanitary and phytosanitary protection does not allow scope for the phased introduction of a new measure, but specific problems are identified by a Member, the Member applying the measure shall upon request enter into consultations with the country with a view to finding a mutually satisfactory solution to the problem while continuing to achieve the importing Member's appropriate level of protection.

3.2   Subject to the conditions specified in paragraph 2 of Annex B to the Agreement on the Application of Sanitary and Phytosanitary Measures, the phrase "reasonable interval" shall be understood to mean normally a period of not less than 6 months. It is understood that timeframes for specific measures have to be considered in the context of the particular circumstances of the measure and actions necessary to implement it. The entry into force of measures which contribute to the liberalization of trade should not be unnecessarily delayed.

3.3   Takes note of the Decision of the Committee on Sanitary and Phytosanitary Measures (G/SPS/19) regarding equivalence, and instructs the Committee to develop expeditiously the specific programme to further the implementation of Article 4 of the Agreement on the Application of Sanitary and Phytosanitary Measures.

3.4   Pursuant to the provisions of Article 12.7 of the Agreement on the Application of Sanitary and Phytosanitary Measures, the Committee on Sanitary and Phytosanitary Measures is instructed to review the operation and implementation of the Agreement on the Application of Sanitary and Phytosanitary Measures at least once every four years.

3.5   (i) Takes note of the actions taken to date by the Director-General to facilitate the increased participation of Members at different levels of development in the work of the relevant international standard setting organizations as well as his efforts to coordinate with these organizations and financial institutions in identifying SPS-related technical assistance needs and how best to address them; and

(ii) urges the Director-General to continue his cooperative efforts with these organizations and institutions in this regard, including with a view to according priority to the effective participation of least-developed countries and facilitating the provision of technical and financial assistance for this purpose.

3.6   (i) Urges Members to provide, to the extent possible, the financial and technical assistance necessary to enable least-developed countries to respond adequately to the introduction of any new SPS measures which may have significant negative effects on their trade; and

(ii) urges Members to ensure that technical assistance is provided to least-developed countries with a view to responding to the special problems faced by them in implementing the Agreement on the Application of Sanitary and Phytosanitary Measures.

4.   Agreement on Textiles and Clothing

Reaffirms the commitment to full and faithful implementation of the Agreement on Textiles and Clothing, and agrees:

4.1   that the provisions of the Agreement relating to the early integration of products and the elimination of quota restrictions should be effectively utilised.

4.2   that Members will exercise particular consideration before initiating investigations in the context of antidumping remedies on textile and clothing exports from developing countries previously subject to quantitative restrictions under the Agreement for a period of two years following full integration of this Agreement into the WTO.

4.3   that without prejudice to their rights and obligations, Members shall notify any changes in their rules of origin concerning products falling under the coverage of the Agreement to the Committee on Rules of Origin which may decide to examine them.

Requests the Council for Trade in Goods to examine the following proposals:

4.4   that when calculating the quota levels for small suppliers for the remaining years of the Agreement, Members will apply the most favourable methodology available in respect of those Members under the growth-on-growth provisions from the beginning of the implementation period; extend the same treatment to least-developed countries; and, where possible, eliminate quota restrictions on imports of such Members;

4.5   that Members will calculate the quota levels for the remaining years of the Agreement with respect to other restrained Members as if implementation of the growth-on-growth provision for stage 3 had been advanced to 1 January 2000;

and make recommendations to the General Council by 31 July 2002 for appropriate action.

5.   **Agreement on Technical Barriers to Trade**

5.1   Confirms the approach to technical assistance being developed by the Committee on Technical Barriers to Trade, reflecting the results of the triennial review work in this area, and mandates this work to continue.

5.2   Subject to the conditions specified in paragraph 12 of Article 2 of the Agreement on Technical Barriers to Trade, the phrase "reasonable interval" shall be understood to mean normally a period of not less than 6 months, except when this would be ineffective in fulfilling the legitimate objectives pursued.

5.3   (i) Takes note of the actions taken to date by the Director-General to facilitate the increased participation of Members at different levels of development in the work of the relevant international standard setting organizations as well as his efforts to coordinate with these organizations and financial institutions in identifying TBT-related technical assistance needs and how best to address them; and

(ii) urges the Director-General to continue his cooperative efforts with these organizations and institutions, including with a view to according priority to the effective participation of least-developed countries and facilitating the provision of technical and financial assistance for this purpose.

5.4   (i) Urges Members to provide, to the extent possible, the financial and technical assistance necessary to enable least-developed countries to respond adequately to the introduction of any new TBT measures which may have significant negative effects on their trade; and

(ii) urges Members to ensure that technical assistance is provided to least-developed countries with a view to responding to the special problems faced by them in implementing the Agreement on Technical Barriers to Trade.

6.   **Agreement on Trade-Related Investment Measures**

6.1   Takes note of the actions taken by the Council for Trade in Goods in regard to requests from some developing-country Members for the extension of the five-year transitional period provided for in Article 5.2 of Agreement on Trade-Related Investment Measures.

6.2   Urges the Council for Trade in Goods to consider positively requests that may be made by least-developed countries under Article 5.3 of the TRIMs Agreement or Article IX.3 of the WTO Agreement, as well as to take into consideration the particular circumstances of least-developed countries when setting the terms and conditions including time-frames.

7.   **Agreement on the Implementation of Article VI of the General Agreement on Tariffs and Trade 1994**

7.1   Agrees that investigating authorities shall examine with special care any application for the initiation of an anti-dumping investigation where an investigation of the same product from the same Member resulted in a negative finding within the 365 days prior to the filing of the application and that, unless this pre-initiation examination indicates that circumstances have changed, the investigation shall not proceed.

7.2   Recognizes that, while Article 15 of the Agreement on the Implementation of Article VI of the General Agreement on Tariffs and Trade 1994 is a mandatory provision, the modalities for its application would benefit from clarification. Accordingly, the Committee on Anti-Dumping Practices is instructed, through its working group on Implementation, to examine this issue and to draw up appropriate recommendations within twelve months on how to operationalize this provision.

7.3   Takes note that Article 5.8 of the Agreement on the Implementation of Article VI of the General Agreement on Tariffs and Trade 1994 does not specify the time-frame to be used in determining the volume of dumped imports, and that this lack of specificity creates uncertainties in the implementation of the provision. The Committee on Anti-Dumping Practices is instructed, through its working group on Implementation, to study this issue and draw up recommendations within 12 months, with a view to ensuring the maximum possible predictability and objectivity in the application of time frames.

7.4   Takes note that Article 18.6 of the Agreement on the Implementation of Article VI of the General Agreement on Tariffs and Trade 1994 requires the Committee on Anti-Dumping Practices to review annually the implementation and operation of the Agreement taking into account the objectives thereof. The Committee on Anti-dumping Practices is instructed to draw up guidelines for the improvement of annual reviews and to report its views and recommendations to the General Council for subsequent decision within 12 months.

8.   Agreement on the Implementation of Article VII of the General Agreement on Tariffs and Trade 1994

8.1   Takes note of the actions taken by the Committee on Customs Valuation in regard to the requests from a number of developing-country Members for the extension of the five-year transitional period provided for in Article 20.1 of Agreement on the Implementation of Article VII of the General Agreement on Tariffs and Trade 1994.

8.2   Urges the Council for Trade in Goods to give positive consideration to requests that may be made by least-developed country Members under paragraphs 1 and 2 of Annex III of the Customs Valuation Agreement or under Article IX.3 of the WTO Agreement, as well as to take into consideration the particular circumstances of least-developed countries when setting the terms and conditions including time-frames.

8.3   Underlines the importance of strengthening cooperation between the customs administrations of Members in the prevention of customs fraud. In this regard, it is agreed that, further to the 1994 Ministerial Decision Regarding Cases Where Customs Administrations Have Reasons to Doubt the Truth or Accuracy of the Declared Value, when the customs administration of an importing Member has reasonable grounds to doubt the truth or accuracy of the declared value, it may seek assistance from the customs administration of an exporting Member on the value of the good concerned. In such cases, the exporting Member shall offer cooperation and assistance, consistent with its domestic laws and procedures, including furnishing information on the export value of the good concerned. Any information provided in this context shall be treated in accordance with Article 10 of the Customs Valuation Agreement. Furthermore, recognizing the legitimate concerns expressed by the customs administrations of several importing Members on the accuracy of the declared value, the Committee on Customs Valuation is directed to identify and assess practical means to address such concerns, including the exchange of information on export values and to report to the General Council by the end of 2002 at the latest.

9. Agreement on Rules of Origin

9.1 Takes note of the report of the Committee on Rules of Origin (G/RO/48) regarding progress on the harmonization work programme, and urges the Committee to complete its work by the end of 2001.

9.2 Agrees that any interim arrangements on rules of origin implemented by Members in the transitional period before the entry into force of the results of the harmonisation work programme shall be consistent with the Agreement on Rules of Origin, particularly Articles 2 and 5 thereof. Without prejudice to Members' rights and obligations, such arrangements may be examined by the Committee on Rules of Origin.

10. Agreement on Subsidies and Countervailing Measures

10.1 Agrees that Annex VII(b) to the Agreement on Subsidies and Countervailing Measures includes the Members that are listed therein until their GNP per capita reaches US $1,000 in constant 1990 dollars for three consecutive years. This decision will enter into effect upon the adoption by the Committee on Subsidies and Countervailing Measures of an appropriate methodology for calculating constant 1990 dollars. If, however, the Committee on Subsidies and Countervailing Measures does not reach a consensus agreement on an appropriate methodology by 1 January 2003, the methodology proposed by the Chairman of the Committee set forth in G/SCM/38, Appendix 2 shall be applied. A Member shall not leave Annex VII(b) so long as its GNP per capita in current dollars has not reached US $1000 based upon the most recent data from the World Bank.

10.2   Takes note of the proposal to treat measures implemented by developing countries with a view to achieving legitimate development goals, such as regional growth, technology research and development funding, production diversification and development and implementation of environmentally sound methods of production as non-actionable subsidies, and agrees that this issue be addressed in accordance with paragraph 13 below. During the course of the negotiations, Members are urged to exercise due restraint with respect to challenging such measures.

10.3   Agrees that the Committee on Subsidies and Countervailing Measures shall continue its review of the provisions of the Agreement on Subsidies and Countervailing Measures regarding countervailing duty investigations and report to the General Council by 31 July 2002.

10.4   Agrees that if a Member has been excluded from the list in paragraph (b) of Annex VII to the Agreement on Subsidies and Countervailing Measures, it shall be re-included in it when its GNP per capita falls back below US$ 1,000.

10.5   Subject to the provisions of Articles 27.5 and 27.6, it is reaffirmed that least-developed country Members are exempt from the prohibition on export subsidies set forth in Article 3.1(a) of the Agreement on Subsidies and Countervailing Measures, and thus have flexibility to finance their exporters, consistent with their development needs. It is understood that the eight-year period in Article 27.5 within which a least-developed country Member must phase out its export subsidies in respect of a product in which it is export-competitive begins from the date export competitiveness exists within the meaning of Article 27.6.

10.6   Having regard to the particular situation of certain developing-country Members, directs the Committee on Subsidies and Countervailing Measures to extend the transition period, under the rubric of Article 27.4 of the Agreement on Subsidies and Countervailing Measures, for certain export subsidies provided by such Members, pursuant to the procedures set forth in document G/SCM/39. Furthermore, when considering a request for an extension of the transition period under the rubric of Article 27.4 of the Agreement on Subsidies and Countervailing Measures, and in order to avoid that Members at similar stages of development and having a similar order of magnitude of share in world trade are treated differently in terms of receiving such extensions for the same eligible programmes and the length of such extensions, directs the Committee to extend the transition period for those developing countries, after taking into account the relative competitiveness in relation to other developing-country Members who have requested extension of the transition period following the procedures set forth in document G/SCM/39.

11. **Agreement on Trade-Related Aspects of Intellectual Property Rights (TRIPS)**

11.1 The TRIPS Council is directed to continue its examination of the scope and modalities for complaints of the types provided for under subparagraphs 1(b) and 1(c) of Article XXIII of GATT 1994 and make recommendations to the Fifth Session of the Ministerial Conference. It is agreed that, in the meantime, Members will not initiate such complaints under the TRIPS Agreement.

11.2 Reaffirming that the provisions of Article 66.2 of the TRIPS Agreement are mandatory, it is agreed that the TRIPS Council shall put in place a mechanism for ensuring the monitoring and full implementation of the obligations in question. To this end, developed-country Members shall submit prior to the end of 2002 detailed reports on the functioning in practice of the incentives provided to their enterprises for the transfer of technology in pursuance of their commitments under Article 66.2. These submissions shall be subject to a review in the TRIPS Council and information shall be updated by Members annually.

12. **Cross-cutting Issues**

12.1 The Committee on Trade and Development is instructed:

(i) to identify those special and differential treatment provisions that are already mandatory in nature and those that are non-binding in character, to consider the legal and practical implications for developed and developing Members of converting special and differential treatment measures into mandatory provisions, to identify those that Members consider should be made mandatory, and to report to the General Council with clear recommendations for a decision by July 2002;

(ii)   to examine additional ways in which special and differential treatment provisions can be made more effective, to consider ways, including improved information flows, in which developing countries, in particular the least-developed countries, may be assisted to make best use of special and differential treatment provisions, and to report to the General Council with clear recommendations for a decision by July 2002; and

(iii)   to consider, in the context of the work programme adopted at the Fourth Session of the Ministerial Conference, how special and differential treatment may be incorporated into the architecture of WTO rules.

The work of the Committee on Trade and Development in this regard shall take fully into consideration previous work undertaken as noted in WT/COMTD/W/77/Rev.1. It will also be without prejudice to work in respect of implementation of WTO Agreements in the General Council and in other Councils and Committees.

12.2   Reaffirms that preferences granted to developing countries pursuant to the Decision of the Contracting Parties of 28 November 1979 ("Enabling Clause")[1] should be generalised, non-reciprocal and non-discriminatory.

13.   **Outstanding Implementation Issues**[2]

Agrees that outstanding implementation issues be addressed in accordance with paragraph 12 of the Ministerial Declaration (WT/MIN(01)/DEC/1).

14.   **Final Provisions**

Requests the Director-General, consistent with paragraphs 38 to 43 of the Ministerial Declaration (WT/MIN(01)/DEC/1), to ensure that WTO technical assistance focuses, on a priority basis, on assisting developing countries to implement existing WTO obligations as well as on increasing their capacity to participate more effectively in future multilateral trade negotiations. In carrying out this mandate, the WTO Secretariat should cooperate more closely with international and regional intergovernmental organisations so as to increase efficiency and synergies and avoid duplication of programmes.

Notes

[1] BISD 26S/203.

[2] A list of these issues is compiled in document Job(01)/152/Rev.1.

Ministerial Decision on the Waiver for the EU-ACP Partnership Agreement

WT/MIN(01)/15

14 November 2001

(01-5786)

MINISTERIAL CONFERENCE
Fourth Session
Doha, 9–14 November 2001

EUROPEAN COMMUNITIES - THE ACP-EC
PARTNERSHIP AGREEMENT
Decision of 14 November 2001

The Ministerial Conference,

Having regard to paragraphs 1 and 3 of Article IX of the Marrakech Agreement Establishing the World Trade Organisation (the "WTO Agreement"), the Guiding Principles to be followed in considering applications for waivers adopted on 1 November 1956 (BISD 5S/25), the Understanding in Respect to Waivers of Obligations under the General Agreement on Tariffs and Trade 1994, paragraph 3 of Article IX of the WTO Agreement, and Decision-Making Procedures under Articles IX and XII of the WTO Agreement agreed by the General Council (WT/L/93);

Taking note of the request of the European Communities (EC) and of the Governments of the ACP States which are also WTO members (hereinafter also the "Parties to the Agreement") for a waiver from the obligations of the European Communities under paragraph 1 of Article I of the General Agreement with respect to the granting of preferential tariff treatment for products originating in ACP States as required by Article 36.3, Annex V and its Protocols of the ACP-EC Partnership Agreement (hereinafter also referred to as "the Agreement")[1];

Considering that, in the field of trade, the provisions of the ACP-EC Partnership Agreement requires preferential tariff treatment by the EC of exports of products originating in the ACP States;

Considering that the Agreement is aimed at improving the standard of living and economic development of the ACP States, including the least developed among them;

Considering also that the preferential tariff treatment for products originating in ACP States as required by Article 36.3, Annex V and its Protocols of the Agreement is designed to promote the expansion of trade and economic development of beneficiaries in a manner consistent with the objectives of the WTO and with the trade, financial and development needs of the beneficiaries and not to raise undue barriers or to create undue difficulties for the trade of other members;

Considering that the Agreement establishes a preparatory period extending until 31 December 2007, by the end of which new trading arrangements shall be concluded between the Parties to the Agreement;

Considering that the trade provisions of the Agreement have been applied since 1 March 2000 on the basis of transitional measures adopted by the ACP-EC joint institutions;

Noting the assurances given by the Parties to the Agreement that they will, upon request, promptly enter into consultations with any interested member with respect to any difficulty or matter that may arise as a result of the implementation of the preferential tariff treatment for products originating in ACP States as required by Article 36.3, Annex V and its Protocols of the Agreement;

Noting that the tariff applied to bananas imported in the "A" and "B" quotas shall not exceed 75 €/tonne until the entry into force of the new EC tariff-only regime.

Noting that the implementation of the preferential tariff treatment for bananas may be affected as a result of GATT Article XXVIII negotiations;

Noting the assurances from the Parties to the Agreement that any re-binding of the EC tariff on bananas under the relevant GATT Article XXVIII procedures should result in at least maintaining total market access for MFN banana suppliers and their willingness to accept a multilateral control on the implementation of this commitment.

Considering that, in light of the foregoing, the exceptional circumstances justifying a waiver from paragraph 1 of Article I of the General Agreement exist;

Decides as follows:

1.   Subject to the terms and conditions set out hereunder, Article I, paragraph 1 of the General Agreement shall be waived, until 31 December 2007, to the extent necessary to permit the European Communities to provide preferential tariff treatment for products originating in ACP States as required by Article 36.3, Annex V and its Protocols of the

ACP-EC Partnership Agreement,[2] without being required to extend the same preferential treatment to like products of any other member.

2.   The Parties to the Agreement shall promptly notify the General Council of any changes in the preferential tariff treatment to products originating in ACP States as required by the relevant provisions of the Agreement covered by this waiver.

3.   The Parties to the Agreement will, upon request, promptly enter into consultations with any interested member with respect to any difficulty or matter that may arise as a result of the implementation of the preferential tariff treatment for products originating in ACP States as required by Article 36.3, Annex V and its Protocols of the Agreement; where a member considers that any benefit accruing to it under the General Agreement may be or is being impaired unduly as a result of such implementation, such consultations shall examine the possibility of action for a satisfactory adjustment of the matter.

3bis   With respect to bananas, the additional provisions in the Annex shall apply.

4.   Any member which considers that the preferential tariff treatment for products originating in ACP States as required by Article 36.3, Annex V and its Protocols of the Agreement is being applied inconsistently with this waiver or that any benefit accruing to it under the General Agreement may be or is being impaired unduly as a result of the implementation of the preferential tariff treatment for products originating in ACP States as required by Article 36.3, Annex V and its Protocols of the Agreement and that consultations have proved unsatisfactory, may bring the matter before the General Council, which will examine it promptly and will formulate any recommendations that they judge appropriate.

5.   The Parties to the Agreement will submit to the General Council an annual report on the implementation of the preferential tariff treatment for products originating in ACP States as required by Article 36.3, Annex V and its Protocols of the Agreement.

6.   This waiver shall not preclude the right of affected members to have recourse to Articles XXII and XXIII of the General Agreement.

Notes

[1] As contained in documents G/C/W/187, G/C/W/204, G/C/W/254 and G/C/W/269).

[2] Any reference to the Partnership Agreement in this Decision shall also include the period during which the trade provisions of this Agreement are applied on the basis of transitional measures adopted by the ACP-EC joint institutions.

ANNEX

The waiver would apply for ACP products under the Cotonou Agreement until 31 December 2007. In the case of bananas, the waiver will also apply until 31 December 2007, subject to the following, which is without prejudice to rights and obligations under Article XXVIII.

- The parties to the Cotonou Agreement will initiate consultations with Members exporting to the EU on a MFN basis (interested parties) early enough to finalize the process of consultations under the procedures hereby established at least three months before the entry into force of the new EC tariff only regime.

- No later than 10 days after the conclusion of Article XXVIII negotiations, interested parties will be informed of the EC intentions concerning the rebinding of the EC tariff on bananas. In the course of such consultations, the EC will provide information on the methodology used for such rebinding. In this regard, all EC WTO market-access commitments relating to bananas should be taken into account.

- Within 60 days of such an announcement, any such interested party may request arbitration.

- The arbitrator shall be appointed within 10 days, following the request subject to agreement between the two parties, failing which the arbitrator shall be appointed by the Director-General of the WTO, following consultations with the parties, within 30 days of the arbitration request. The mandate of the arbitrator shall be to determine, within 90 days of his appointment, whether the envisaged rebinding of the EC tariff on bananas would result in at least maintaining total market access for MFN banana suppliers, taking into account the above-mentioned EC commitments.

- If the arbitrator determines that the rebinding would not result in at least maintaining total market access for MFN suppliers, the EC shall rectify the matter. Within 10 days of the notification of the arbitration award to the

General Council, the EC will enter into consultations with those interested parties that requested the arbitration. In the absence of a mutually satisfactory solution, the same arbitrator will be asked to determine, within 30 days of the new arbitration request, whether the EC has rectified the matter. The second arbitration award will be notified to the General Council. If the EC has failed to rectify the matter, this waiver shall cease to apply to bananas upon entry into force of the new EC tariff regime. The Article XXVIII negotiations and the arbitration procedures shall be concluded before the entry into force of the new EC tariff only regime on 1 January 2006.

Ministerial Decision on the EU's Transitional Regime for Banana Imports

WT/MIN(01)/16
14 November 2001
(01–5787)

MINISTERIAL CONFERENCE
Fourth Session
Doha, 9–14 November 2001

EUROPEAN COMMUNITIES – TRANSITIONAL REGIME FOR THE EC AUTONOMOUS TARIFF RATE QUOTAS ON IMPORTS OF BANANAS
Decision of 14 November 2001

The Ministerial Conference,

Having regard to the Guiding Principles to be followed in considering applications for waivers adopted on 1 November 1956, the Understanding in Respect of Waivers of Obligations under the General Agreement on Tariffs and Trade 1994, and paragraphs 3 and 4 of Article IX of the Marrakesh Agreement Establishing the World Trade Organization (hereinafter "WTO Agreement");

Taking note of the request of the European Communities for a waiver from its obligations under paragraphs 1 and 2 of Article XIII of the GATT 1994 with respect to bananas;

Taking note of the understandings reached by the EC, Ecuador and the United States that identify the means by which the longstanding dispute over the EC's banana regime can be resolved, in particular their provision for a temporary global quota allocation for ACP banana supplying countries under specified conditions;

Taking into account the exceptional circumstances surrounding the resolution of the bananas dispute and the interests of many WTO Members in the EC banana regime;

Recognizing the need to afford sufficient protection to the ACP banana supplying countries, including the most vulnerable, during a limited transition period, to enable them to prepare for a tariff-only regime;

Noting assurances given by the EC that it will, upon request, promptly enter into consultations with any interested member with respect to any difficulty or matter that may arise as a result of the implementation of the tariff rate quota for bananas originating in ACP States;

Considering that, in light of the foregoing, the exceptional circumstances justifying a waiver from paragraphs 1 and 2 of Article XIII of the GATT 1994 with respect to bananas exist;

Decides as follows:

1.   With respect to the EC's imports of bananas, as of 1 January 2002, and until 31 December 2005, paragraphs 1 and 2 of Article XIII of the GATT 1994 are waived with respect to the EC's separate tariff quota of 750,000 tonnes for bananas of ACP origin.

2.   The EC will, upon request, promptly enter into consultations with any interested member with respect to any difficulty or matter that may arise as a result of the implementation of the separate tariff rate quota for bananas originating in ACP States covered by this waiver; where a Member considers that any benefit accruing to it under the GATT 1994 may be or is being impaired unduly as a result of such implementation, such consultations shall examine the possibility of action for a satisfactory adjustment of the matter.

3.   Any Member which considers that the separate tariff rate quota for bananas originating in ACP States covered by this waiver is being applied inconsistently with this waiver or that any benefit accruing to it under the GATT 1994 may be or is being impaired unduly as a result of the implementation of the separate tariff rate quota for bananas originating in ACP States covered by this waiver and that consultations have proved unsatisfactory, may bring the matter before the General Council, which will examine it promptly and will formulate any recommendations that they judge appropriate.

4.   This waiver shall not preclude the right of affected members to have recourse to Articles XXII and XXIII of the GATT 1994.

Procedures for extending provisions allowing some developing countries to continue to subsidize exports

This comes under paragraph 10.6 of the Doha Implementation Decision, and refers to Article 27.4 of the Subsidies Agreement. The procedure is issued by the Subsidies and Countervailing Measures Committee, which met specially for the purpose at the Doha Ministerial Conference. The decision was adopted on 14 November 2001, along with the Doha ministerial declarations and decisions.

G/SCM/39
20 November 2001
(01-5767)

**Committee on Subsidies
and Countervailing Measures**

PROCEDURES FOR EXTENSIONS UNDER ARTICLE 27.4
FOR CERTAIN DEVELOPING COUNTRY MEMBERS

The Committee on Subsidies and Countervailing Measures ("SCM Committee") shall follow the procedures set forth below in respect of extensions of the transition period under Article 27.4 of the Agreement on Subsidies and Countervailing Measures ("SCM Agreement") for certain developing country Members. The programmes to which these procedures shall apply are those meeting the criteria set forth in 2.

1.   Mechanism for extension

(a)   A Member that maintains programmes meeting the criteria set forth in 2 and that wishes to make use of these procedures, shall initiate Article 27.4 consultations with the Committee in respect of an extension for its eligible subsidy programmes as referred to in 2, on the basis of documentation to be submitted to the Committee not later than 31 December 2001. This documentation shall consist of (i) an identification by the Member of those programmes for which it is seeking an extension under SCM Article 27.4 pursuant to these procedures; and (ii) a statement that the extension is necessary in the light of the Member's economic, financial and development needs.

(b)   Not later than 28 February 2002, the Member seeking an extension shall submit to the SCM Committee an initial notification as referred to in 3(a) providing detailed information about the programmes for which extension is being sought.

(c)   Following receipt of the notifications referred to in 1(b), the SCM Committee shall consider those notifications, with an opportunity for Members to seek clarification of the notified information and/or additional detail with a view to understanding the nature and operation of the notified programmes, and their scope, coverage and intensity of benefits, as referred to in 3(b). The purpose of this consideration by the SCM Committee shall be to verify that the programmes are of the type eligible under these procedures as referred to in 2, and that the transparency requirement referred to in 3(a) and 3(b) is fulfilled. Not later than 15 December 2002, Members of the SCM Committee shall grant extensions for calendar year 2003 for those programmes notified pursuant to these procedures, provided that the notified programmes meet the eligibility criteria in 2 and that the transparency requirement is fulfilled. The notified information on the basis of which the extensions are granted, including information provided in response to requests from Members as referred to above, shall form the frame of reference for the annual reviews of the extensions as referred to in 1(d) and 1(e).

(d)   As provided for in SCM Article 27.4, the extensions granted by the SCM Committee pursuant to these procedures shall be subject to annual review in the form of consultations between the Committee and the Members receiving the extensions. These annual reviews shall be conducted on the basis of updating notifications from the Members in question, as referred to in 3(a) and 3(b). The purpose of the annual reviews shall be to ensure that the transparency and standstill requirements as set forth in 3 and 4 are being fulfilled.

(e)   Through the end of calendar year 2007, subject to annual reviews during that period to verify that the transparency and standstill requirements set forth in 3 and 4 are being fulfilled, Members of the Committee shall agree to continue the extensions granted pursuant to 1(c).

(f)   During the last year of the period referred to in 1(e), a Member that has received an extension under these procedures shall have the possibility to seek a continuation of the extension pursuant to SCM Article 27.4, for the programmes in question. The Committee shall consider any such requests at that year's annual review, on the basis of the provisions of SCM Article 27.4, i.e., outside the framework of these procedures.

(g)   If a continuation of the extension pursuant to 1(f) is either not requested or not granted, the Member in question shall have the final two years referred to in the last sentence of SCM Article 27.4.

2.   Eligible programmes

Programmes eligible for extension pursuant to these procedures, and for which Members shall therefore grant extensions for calendar year 2003 as referred to in 1(c), are export subsidy programmes (i) in the form of full or partial exemptions from import duties and internal taxes, (ii) which were in existence not later than 1 September 2001, and (iii) which are provided by developing country Members (iv) whose share of world merchandise export trade was not greater than 0.10 per cent[1], (v) whose total Gross National Income ("GNI") for the year 2000 as published by the World Bank was at or below US $20 billion[2], (vi) and who are otherwise eligible to request an extension pursuant to Article 27.4[3], and (vii) in respect of which these procedures are followed.

3.   Transparency

(a)   The initial notification referred to in 1(b), and the updating notifications referred to in 1(d), shall follow the agreed format for subsidy notifications under SCM Article 25 (found in G/SCM/6).

(b)   During the SCM Committee's consideration/review of the notifications referred to in 1(c) and 1(d), notifying Members can be requested by other Members to provide additional detail and clarification, with a view to confirming that the programmes meet the criteria set forth in 2, and to establishing transparency in respect of the scope, coverage and intensity of benefits (the "favourability") of the programmes in question[4]. Any information provided in response to such requests shall be considered part of the notified information.

4.   Standstill

(a)   The programmes for which an extension is granted shall not be modified during the period of extension referred to in 1(e) so as to make them more favourable than they were as at 1 September 2001. The continuation of an expiring programme without modification shall not be deemed to violate standstill.

(b) The scope, coverage and intensity of benefits (the "favourability") of the programmes as at 1 September 2001 shall be specified in the initial notification referred to in 1(b), and standstill as referred to in 4(a) shall be verified on the basis of the notified information referred to in 1(d) and 3(b).

5. Product graduation on the basis of export competitiveness

Notwithstanding these procedures, Articles 27.5 and 27.6 shall apply in respect of export subsidies for which extensions are granted pursuant to these procedures.

6. Members listed in Annex VII(b)

(a) A Member listed in Annex VII(b) whose GNP per capita has reached the level provided for in that Annex and whose programme(s) meet the criteria in 2 shall be eligible to make use of these procedures.

(b) A Member listed in Annex VII(b) whose GNP per capita has not reached the level provided for in that Annex and whose programme(s) meet the criteria in 2 may reserve its right to make use of these procedures, as referred to in 6(c), by submitting the documentation referred to in 1(a) not later than 31 December 2001.

(c) If the per capita GNP of a Member referred to in 6(b) reaches the level provided for in that Annex during the period referred to in 1(e), that Member shall be able to make use of these procedures as from the date at which its per capita GNP reaches that level and for the remainder of the period referred to in 1(e), as well as for any additional periods as referred to in 1(f) and 1(g), subject to the remaining provisions of these procedures.

(d) For a Member referred to in 6(b), the effective date for the standstill requirement referred to in 4(a) shall be the year in which that Member's GNP per capita reaches the level provided for in Annex VII(b).

7. Final provisions

(a) The decision by Ministers, these procedures, and the SCM Article 27.4 extensions granted thereunder, are without prejudice to any requests for extensions under Article 27.4 that are not made pursuant to these procedures.

(b)   The decision by Ministers, these procedures, and the SCM Article 27.4 extensions granted thereunder, shall not affect any other existing rights and obligations under SCM Article 27.4 or under other provisions of the SCM Agreement.

(c)   The criteria set forth in these procedures are solely and strictly for the purpose of determining whether Members are eligible to invoke these procedures. Members of the Committee agree that these criteria have no precedential value or relevance, direct or indirect, for any other purpose.

Notes

[1]   According to the calculations performed by the WTO Secretariat as reflected in Appendix 3 to the Report of the Chairman (G/SCM/38).

[2]   The SCM Committee shall consider other appropriate data sources in respect of Members for whom the World Bank does not publish total GNI data.

[3]   The fact that a Member is listed in Annex VII(b) shall not be deemed to make that Member otherwise ineligible to request an extension pursuant to Article 27.4.

[4]   The scope, coverage and intensity of the programmes in question will be determined on the basis of the legal instruments underlying the programmes.

Organization of work

Geneva 2002

- General Council chairperson's statement

General Council Chairperson's statement including principles and practices for the negotiations

TN/C/1
4 February 2002
(02-0530)

Trade Negotiations Committee
1 February 2002

STATEMENT BY THE CHAIRMAN OF THE GENERAL COUNCIL

The following statement was made by the Chairman of the General Council at the first meeting of the Trade Negotiations Committee on 1 February 2002. At that meeting, the Trade Negotiations Committee took note of the statement and endorsed the Principles and Practices set out in Section B.

A.   Introductory Comments

First of all I should emphasize that the mandate for the TNC, as for the negotiations as a whole, is that agreed by Ministers at Doha in November 2001 and set out in their Ministerial Declaration - paragraphs 45 to 52 of that Declaration in particular relate to the TNC which Ministers have established under the authority of the General Council to supervise the overall conduct of the negotiations. It shall establish appropriate negotiating mechanisms as required and supervise the progress of the negotiations. Other specific functions are set out elsewhere in the Declaration, for example in relation to implementation issues.

That is the mandate. Our task is to give effect to it efficiently and promptly. It is in this spirit that I have considered the suggestions by a number of delegations concerning possible guidance to assist the TNC's work. Clearly, any such guidance should help the TNC to fulfil its mandate, not make it more difficult. This said, it may assist delegations if I set out my understanding, derived from the extensive consultations I have held, of some basic principles and practices which I believe it is widely felt we should keep in mind as the TNC carries out its work under its Ministerial Mandate. This statement will, of course, be reflected in the minutes of the TNC and also circulated as a TNC document.

I hope it will provide some assurance to delegations that we are all committed to seeing the work of the TNC and the negotiations it supervises conducted according to the best WTO practices and in a transparent, inclusive and accountable manner. In keeping with usual WTO practice, the TNC should follow the General Council's Rules of Procedure *mutatis mutandis*, i.e. with only such adjustments as may be found necessary.

I should like to note that in my consultations a wide variety of views have been expressed, and I am grateful to delegations for the cooperative and constructive spirit they have shown throughout. While I have carefully considered and attempted to reflect delegations' views in my statement, I must stress that this is not a fully negotiated text. Delegations will of course have the opportunity under Item 4 of the Agenda to express their views and understandings of the sense of the points I am putting forward in summary here. I should, however, like to note in particular the view expressed by a number of delegations that the proposed appointment of the Director-General *ex officio* as Chairman of the TNC under Item 1 of the Agenda is an exceptional arrangement and that appointments to WTO bodies should normally be made from among representatives of WTO Members.

B.   Principles and Practices

General Council Authority

- In line with the Doha Ministerial Declaration, the TNC has been established by Ministers under the authority of the General Council with the mandate of supervising the overall conduct of the negotiations. The TNC and its negotiating bodies do not constitute a parallel or competing machinery to the existing WTO bodies.

- The General Council is in charge of the WTO's work programme as a whole, including that set out in the Doha Declaration. The TNC should report to each regular meeting of the General Council. The General Council retains the overall responsibility for the preparations for Ministerial Conferences.

Transparency and Process

- The Ministerial Declaration sets out that the negotiations shall be conducted in a transparent manner among participants, in order to facilitate the effective participation of all.

- In its own work, and also in its supervision of the conduct of the negotiations, the TNC should build on the best practices established over the past two years with regard to internal transparency and participation of all Members. These practices were articulated by my predecessor, Ambassador Bryn, on 17 July 2000 (document WT/GC/M/57) as a reflection of the mainstream of the extensive discussions on internal transparency.

- Minutes of meetings of the TNC and of negotiating bodies should be circulated expeditiously and in all three official languages at the same time. Furthermore, the

Secretariat is urged to take all possible steps to ensure the prompt and efficient dissemination of information relating to negotiations to non-resident and smaller missions in particular.

- The constraints of smaller delegations should be taken into account when scheduling meetings. The TNC will keep the calendar of meetings under surveillance. As an overall guideline, as far as possible only one negotiating body should meet at the same time. The TNC should consider how this arrangement should be supervised.

Chairpersons of the TNC and Negotiating Bodies

- Chairpersons should be impartial and objective, and discharge their duties in accordance with the mandate conferred on the TNC by Ministers.

- Chairpersons should ensure transparency and inclusiveness in decision-making and consultative processes taking into account the intergovernmental and Member-driven character of the WTO.

- Chairpersons should aim to facilitate consensus among participants and should seek to evolve consensus texts through the negotiation process.

- In their regular reporting to overseeing bodies, Chairpersons should reflect consensus, or where this is not possible, different positions on issues.

- The General Council should ensure that suitable arrangements are made to promote continuity in the work of the TNC during the transition from the current to the next Director-General.

- The Chairperson of the TNC should work in close cooperation with the Chairperson of the General Council and the Chairpersons of the negotiating bodies.

C.   Proposals for Action by the TNC

- I propose that the TNC take note of my statement and endorse the Principles and Practices set out in Section B of that statement.

Agenda Item 1

- I propose that the TNC appoint the Director-General in an *ex officio* capacity to chair the TNC until the deadline of 1 January 2005 established in the Doha Declaration. It is understood that doing so does not create a precedent for the future.

Agenda Item 2

I propose that:

- The TNC adopt the following structure:

    - the agriculture and services negotiations will be pursued in Special Sessions of the Committee on Agriculture and the Council for Trade in Services, respectively;

    - negotiations on market access for non-agricultural products will take place in a Negotiating Group on Market Access to be created;

    - negotiations on the establishment of a multilateral system of notification and registration of geographical indications for wines and spirits under the Agreement on Trade-Related Aspects of Intellectual Property Rights will take place in Special Sessions of the TRIPS Council, while other issues in paragraphs 18 and 19 of the Doha Ministerial Declaration relating to TRIPS will be addressed in regular meetings of the TRIPS Council on a priority basis;

    - negotiations on WTO rules will take place in a Negotiating Group on Rules to be created;

    - negotiations on improvements and clarifications to the Dispute Settlement Understanding will take place in Special Sessions of the Dispute Settlement Body;

    - negotiations on trade and environment will take place in Special Sessions of the Committee on Trade and Environment; and

    - negotiations on outstanding implementation issues will take place in the relevant bodies in accordance with the provisions of paragraph 12 of the Doha Ministerial Declaration and of the Decision on Implementation-Related Issues and Concerns of 14 November 2001.

- As reaffirmed by Ministers at Doha, provisions for special and differential treatment are an integral part of the WTO Agreements. The negotiations and other aspects of the work programme shall take fully into account the principle of special and differential treatment for developing and least-developed countries as provided for in paragraph 50 of the Ministerial Declaration. The review of all special and differential treatment provisions with a view to strengthening them and making them more precise, effective and operational provided for in paragraph 44 of the Ministerial Declaration shall be carried out by the Committee on Trade and Development in Special Sessions.

- The Chairman of the General Council consult on the chairmanships of the individual negotiating bodies. Consideration should be given to the overall balance between developed and developing-country candidates, bearing in mind the quality and integrity of each individual.

- The Chairpersons of individual negotiating bodies be appointed to serve up to the Fifth Ministerial Conference, at which time all the appointments will be reviewed. Chairpersons should be selected from among Geneva-based representatives in the majority. Other qualified individuals nominated by Member governments could also be considered. This would have to be on the understanding that these individuals would be available in Geneva as often as needed, and that any related costs would need to be handled in a way which did not disadvantage Members for whom there could be a problem.

Agenda Item 3

- I propose that the TNC develop its own work schedule on the basis of one meeting every 2–3 months, but with provision for more meetings when necessary.

Doha Round texts

After Doha

- 2003 - Services: special treatment for least-developed countries
- 2004 - "Frameworks"
- 2005 - Hong Kong Ministerial Declaration

Hong Kong 2005:
Main picture: Malaysian Trade Minister Rafidah Aziz comments on the final draft declaration.
Inset bottom left: Delegates scrutinize the final draft.
Inset middle: Director-General Pascal Lamy consults Zambian Trade Minister Dipak Patel.
Geneva 2004:
Inset bottom right: Delegates examine the draft frameworks decision.

Services: Modalities for special treatment for least-developed countries

TN/S/13
5 September 2003
(03-4637)

Council for Trade in Services
Special Session

MODALITIES FOR THE SPECIAL TREATMENT FOR LEAST-DEVELOPED COUNTRY MEMBERS IN THE NEGOTIATIONS ON TRADE IN SERVICES
Adopted by the Special Session of the Council for
Trade in Services on 3 September 2003

I.   OBJECTIVES AND PRINCIPLES

1.   In pursuance of the objectives of the GATS and as required by Article XIX:3 of the GATS special treatment for least-developed country Members (LDCs) shall be granted by providing special priority to LDCs in the implementation of paragraphs 1 and 2 of Article IV of the GATS. Particular account shall be taken of the serious difficulty of LDCs in undertaking negotiated specific commitments in view of their special economic situation and their development, trade and financial needs.

2.   The importance of trade in services for LDCs goes beyond pure economic significance due to the major role services play for achieving social and development objectives and as a means of addressing poverty, upgrading welfare, improving universal availability and access to basic services, and in ensuring sustainable development, including its social dimension. LDCs are facing serious difficulty in addressing a number of complex issues simultaneously, and lack institutional and human capacities to analyse and respond to offers and requests. This should be factored into the negotiating process in general and regarding the individual requests made to LDCs.

3.   Together with the Guidelines and Procedures for the Negotiations on Trade in Services (S/L/93), the Modalities for the Special Treatment for Least-Developed Country Members in the Negotiations on Trade in Services shall ensure maximum flexibility for LDCs and shall form the basis for the negotiations.

II.   SCOPE

4.   Members shall take into account the serious difficulty of LDCs in undertaking negotiated specific commitments in view of their special economic situation, and therefore

shall exercise restraint in seeking commitments from LDCs. In particular, they shall generally not seek the removal of conditions which LDCs may attach when making access to their markets available to foreign service suppliers to the extent that those conditions are aimed at achieving the objectives of Article IV of the GATS.

5.　There shall be flexibility for LDCs for opening fewer sectors, liberalizing fewer types of transactions, and progressively extending market access in line with their development situation. LDCs shall not be expected to offer full national treatment, nor are they expected to undertake additional commitments under Article XVIII of the GATS on regulatory issues which may go beyond their institutional, regulatory, and administrative capacities. In response to requests, LDCs may make commitments compatible with their development, trade and financial needs and which are limited in terms of sectors, modes of supply and scope.

6.　Members shall, as provided for in Articles IV and XIX of the GATS, give special priority to providing effective market access in sectors and modes of supply of export interest to LDCs, through negotiated specific commitments pursuant to Parts III and IV of the GATS. LDCs should indicate those sectors and modes of supply that represent priority in their development policies, so that Members take these priorities into account in the negotiations.

7.　Members shall work to develop appropriate mechanisms with a view to achieving full implementation of Article IV:3 of the GATS and facilitating effective access of LDCs' services and service suppliers to foreign markets.

8.　Members shall take measures, in accordance with their individual capacities, aimed at increasing the participation of LDCs in trade in services. Such measures could include:

- strengthening programmes to promote investment in LDCs, with a view to building their domestic services capacity and enhancing their efficiency and export competitiveness;

- reinforcing export/import promotion programmes;

- promoting the development of LDCs' infrastructure and services exports through training, technology transfer, enterprise level actions and schemes, intergovernmental cooperation programmes, and where feasible, financial resources; and

- improving the access of LDCs' services and service suppliers to distribution channels and information networks, especially in sectors and modes of supply of interest to LDCs.

9.   It is recognized that the temporary movement of natural persons supplying services (Mode 4) provides potential benefits to the sending and recipient Members. LDCs have indicated that this is one of the most important means of supplying services internationally. Members shall to the extent possible, and consistently with Article XIX of the GATS, consider undertaking commitments to provide access in mode 4, taking into account all categories of natural persons identified by LDCs in their requests.

10.   LDCs shall be granted appropriate credit for their autonomous trade liberalization. In addition, Members shall refrain from requesting credits from LDCs.

11.   In developing any multilateral rules and disciplines, including under GATS Articles VI:4 (Domestic regulation), X (Emergency safeguard measures), XIII (Government procurement) and XV (Subsidies), Members shall take into account the specific interests and difficulties of LDCs.

III.   PRINCIPLES FOR THE PROVISION OF TECHNICAL ASSISTANCE WITH REGARD TO TRADE IN SERVICES

12.   Targeted and coordinated technical assistance and capacity building programmes shall continue to be provided to LDCs in order to strengthen their domestic services capacity, build institutional and human capacity, and enable them to undertake appropriate regulatory reforms. In pursuance of Paragraph 14 of the Guidelines and Procedures for the Negotiations on Trade in Services (S/L/93), technical assistance shall also be provided to LDCs to carry out national assessments of trade in services in overall terms and on a sectoral basis with reference to the objectives of the GATS and Article IV in particular.

IV.   MECHANISMS AND PROCEDURES

13.   The Special Session of the Council for Trade in Services shall review, as necessary, the implementation of these modalities under the standing item on "Review of Progress in the Negotiations".

14.   In his report to the Trade Negotiations Committee, the Chairman of the Special Session of the Council for Trade in Services will include the issues raised by Members with regard to these modalities.

General Council decision
(the 'July Package' or 2004 'Frameworks')

WT/L/579

2 August 2004

(04-3297)

Doha Work Programme

Decision Adopted by the General Council on 1 August 2004

1.   The General Council reaffirms the Ministerial Declarations and Decisions adopted at Doha and the full commitment of all Members to give effect to them. The Council emphasizes Members' resolve to complete the Doha Work Programme fully and to conclude successfully the negotiations launched at Doha. Taking into account the Ministerial Statement adopted at Cancún on 14 September 2003, and the statements by the Council Chairman and the Director-General at the Council meeting of 15-16 December 2003, the Council takes note of the report by the Chairman of the Trade Negotiations Committee (TNC) and agrees to take action as follows:

   a.   Agriculture: the General Council adopts the framework set out in Annex A to this document.

   b.   Cotton: the General Council reaffirms the importance of the Sectoral Initiative on Cotton and takes note of the parameters set out in Annex A within which the trade-related aspects of this issue will be pursued in the agriculture negotiations. The General Council also attaches importance to the development aspects of the Cotton Initiative and wishes to stress the complementarity between the trade and development aspects. The Council takes note of the recent Workshop on Cotton in Cotonou on 23-24 March 2004 organized by the WTO Secretariat, and other bilateral and multilateral efforts to make progress on the development assistance aspects and instructs the Secretariat to continue to work with the development community and to provide the Council with periodic reports on relevant developments.

   Members should work on related issues of development multilaterally with the international financial institutions, continue their bilateral programmes, and all developed countries are urged to participate. In this regard, the General Council instructs the Director General to consult with the relevant international organizations, including the Bretton Woods Institutions, the Food and Agriculture Organization and the International Trade Centre to direct effectively existing programmes and any additional resources towards development of the economies where cotton has vital importance.

c. **Non-agricultural Market Access**: the General Council adopts the framework set out in Annex B to this document.

d. **Development**:

Principles: development concerns form an integral part of the Doha Ministerial Declaration. The General Council rededicates and recommits Members to fulfilling the development dimension of the Doha Development Agenda, which places the needs and interests of developing and least-developed countries at the heart of the Doha Work Programme. The Council reiterates the important role that enhanced market access, balanced rules, and well targeted, sustainably financed technical assistance and capacity building programmes can play in the economic development of these countries.

Special and Differential Treatment: the General Council reaffirms that provisions for special and differential (S&D) treatment are an integral part of the WTO Agreements. The Council recalls Ministers' decision in Doha to review all S&D treatment provisions with a view to strengthening them and making them more precise, effective and operational. The Council recognizes the progress that has been made so far. The Council instructs the Committee on Trade and Development in Special Session to expeditiously complete the review of all the outstanding Agreement-specific proposals and report to the General Council, with clear recommendations for a decision, by July 2005. The Council further instructs the Committee, within the parameters of the Doha mandate, to address all other outstanding work, including on the cross-cutting issues, the monitoring mechanism and the incorporation of S&D treatment into the architecture of WTO rules, as referred to in TN/CTD/7 and report, as appropriate, to the General Council.

The Council also instructs all WTO bodies to which proposals in Category II have been referred to expeditiously complete the consideration of these proposals and report to the General Council, with clear recommendations for a decision, as soon as possible and no later than July 2005. In doing so these bodies will ensure that, as far as possible, their meetings do not overlap so as to enable full and effective participation of developing countries in these discussions.

Technical Assistance: the General Council recognizes the progress that has been made since the Doha Ministerial Conference in expanding Trade-Related Technical Assistance (TRTA) to developing countries and low-income countries in transition. In furthering this effort the Council affirms that such countries, and in particular least-developed countries, should be provided with enhanced TRTA and capacity building, to increase their effective participation in the negotiations, to facilitate their implementation of WTO rules, and to enable them to adjust and diversify their economies. In this context the Council welcomes and further encourages the improved coordination with other agencies, including under the Integrated Framework for TRTA for the LDCs (IF) and the Joint Integrated Technical Assistance Programme (JITAP).

Implementation: concerning implementation-related issues, the General Council reaffirms the mandates Ministers gave in paragraph 12 of the Doha Ministerial Declaration and the Doha Decision on Implementation-Related Issues and Concerns, and renews Members' determination to find appropriate solutions to outstanding issues. The Council instructs the Trade Negotiations Committee, negotiating bodies and other WTO bodies concerned to redouble their efforts to find appropriate solutions as a priority. Without prejudice to the positions of Members, the Council requests the Director-General to continue with his consultative process on all outstanding implementation issues under paragraph 12(b) of the Doha Ministerial Declaration, including on issues related to the extension of the protection of geographical indications provided for in Article 23 of the TRIPS Agreement to products other than wines and spirits, if need be by appointing Chairpersons of concerned WTO bodies as his Friends and/or by holding dedicated consultations. The Director-General shall report to the TNC and the General Council no later than May 2005. The Council shall review progress and take any appropriate action no later than July 2005.

Other Development Issues: in the ongoing market access negotiations, recognising the fundamental principles of the WTO and relevant provisions of GATT 1994, special attention shall be given to the specific trade and development related needs and concerns of developing countries, including capacity constraints. These particular concerns of developing countries, including relating to food security, rural development, livelihood, preferences, commodities and net food imports, as well as prior unilateral liberalisation, should be taken into consideration, as appropriate, in the course of the Agriculture and NAMA negotiations. The trade-related issues identified for the fuller integration of small, vulnerable economies into the multilateral trading system, should also be addressed, without creating a sub-category of Members, as part of a work programme, as mandated in paragraph 35 of the Doha Ministerial Declaration.

Least-Developed Countries: the General Council reaffirms the commitments made at Doha concerning least-developed countries and renews its determination to fulfil these commitments. Members will continue to take due account of the concerns of least-developed countries in the negotiations. The Council confirms that nothing in this Decision shall detract in any way from the special provisions agreed by Members in respect of these countries.

e.   Services: the General Council takes note of the report to the TNC by the Special Session of the Council for Trade in Services[1] and reaffirms Members' commitment to progress in this area of the negotiations in line with the Doha mandate. The Council adopts the recommendations agreed by the Special Session, set out in Annex C to this document, on the basis of which further progress in the services negotiations will be pursued. Revised offers should be tabled by May 2005.

f.   Other negotiating bodies:

Rules, Trade & Environment and TRIPS: the General Council takes note of the reports to the TNC by the Negotiating Group on Rules and by the Special Sessions of the Committee on Trade and Environment and the TRIPS Council.[2] The Council reaffirms Members' commitment to progress in all of these areas of the negotiations in line with the Doha mandates.

Dispute Settlement: the General Council takes note of the report to the TNC by the Special Session of the Dispute Settlement Body[3] and reaffirms Members' commitment to progress in this area of the negotiations in line with the Doha mandate. The Council adopts the TNC's recommendation that work in the Special Session should continue on the basis set out by the Chairman of that body in his report to the TNC.

g.   Trade Facilitation: taking note of the work done on trade facilitation by the Council for Trade in Goods under the mandate in paragraph 27 of the Doha Ministerial Declaration and the work carried out under the auspices of the General Council both prior to the Fifth Ministerial Conference and after its conclusion, the

General Council decides by explicit consensus to commence negotiations on the basis of the modalities set out in Annex D to this document.

Relationship between Trade and Investment, Interaction between Trade and Competition Policy and Transparency in Government Procurement: the Council agrees that these issues, mentioned in the Doha Ministerial Declaration in paragraphs 20-22, 23-25 and 26 respectively, will not form part of the Work Programme set out in that Declaration and therefore no work towards negotiations on any of these issues will take place within the WTO during the Doha Round.

h.   Other elements of the Work Programme: the General Council reaffirms the high priority Ministers at Doha gave to those elements of the Work Programme which do not involve negotiations. Noting that a number of these issues are of particular interest to developing-country Members, the Council emphasizes its commitment to fulfil the mandates given by Ministers in all these areas. To this end, the General Council and other relevant bodies shall report in line with their Doha mandates to the Sixth Session of the Ministerial Conference. The moratoria covered by paragraph 11.1 of the Doha Ministerial Decision on Implementation-related Issues and Concerns and paragraph 34 of the Doha Ministerial Declaration are extended up to the Sixth Ministerial Conference.

2.   The General Council agrees that this Decision and its Annexes shall not be used in any dispute settlement proceeding under the DSU and shall not be used for interpreting the existing WTO Agreements.

3.   The General Council calls on all Members to redouble their efforts towards the conclusion of a balanced overall outcome of the Doha Development Agenda in fulfilment of the commitments Ministers took at Doha. The Council agrees to continue the negotiations launched at Doha beyond the timeframe set out in paragraph 45 of the Doha Declaration, leading to the Sixth Session of the Ministerial Conference. Recalling its decision of 21 October 2003 to accept the generous offer of the Government of Hong Kong, China to host the Sixth Session, the Council further agrees that this Session will be held in December 2005.

Notes

[1]   This report is contained in document TN/S/16.

[2]   The reports to the TNC referenced in this paragraph are contained in the following documents: Negotiating Group on Rules - TN/RL/9; Special Session of the Committee on Trade and Environment - TN/TE/9; Special Session of the Council for TRIPS - TN/IP/10.

[3]   This report is contained in document TN/DS/10.

Annex A

Framework for Establishing Modalities in Agriculture

1.   The starting point for the current phase of the agriculture negotiations has been the mandate set out in Paragraph 13 of the Doha Ministerial Declaration. This in turn built on the long-term objective of the Agreement on Agriculture to establish a fair and market-oriented trading system through a programme of fundamental reform. The elements below offer the additional precision required at this stage of the negotiations and thus the basis for the negotiations of full modalities in the next phase. The level of ambition set by the Doha mandate will continue to be the basis for the negotiations on agriculture.

2.   The final balance will be found only at the conclusion of these subsequent negotiations and within the Single Undertaking. To achieve this balance, the modalities to be developed will need to incorporate operationally effective and meaningful provisions for special and differential treatment for developing country Members. Agriculture is of critical importance to the economic development of developing country Members and they must be able to pursue agricultural policies that are supportive of their development goals, poverty reduction strategies, food security and livelihood concerns. Non-trade concerns, as referred to in Paragraph 13 of the Doha Declaration, will be taken into account.

3.   The reforms in all three pillars form an interconnected whole and must be approached in a balanced and equitable manner.

4.   The General Council recognizes the importance of cotton for a certain number of countries and its vital importance for developing countries, especially LDCs. It will be addressed ambitiously, expeditiously, and specifically, within the agriculture negotiations. The provisions of this framework provide a basis for this approach, as does the sectoral initiative on cotton. The Special Session of the Committee on Agriculture shall ensure appropriate prioritization of the cotton issue independently from other sectoral initiatives. A subcommittee on cotton will meet periodically and report to the Special Session of the Committee on Agriculture to review progress. Work shall encompass all trade-distorting policies affecting the sector in all three pillars of market access, domestic support, and export competition, as specified in the Doha text and this Framework text.

5.   Coherence between trade and development aspects of the cotton issue will be pursued as set out in paragraph 1.b of the text to which this Framework is annexed.

DOMESTIC SUPPORT

6.   The Doha Ministerial Declaration calls for "substantial reductions in trade-distorting domestic support". With a view to achieving these substantial reductions, the negotiations in this pillar will ensure the following:

- Special and differential treatment remains an integral component of domestic support. Modalities to be developed will include longer implementation periods and lower reduction coefficients for all types of trade-distorting domestic support and continued access to the provisions under Article 6.2.

- There will be a strong element of harmonisation in the reductions made by developed Members. Specifically, higher levels of permitted trade-distorting domestic support will be subject to deeper cuts.

- Each such Member will make a substantial reduction in the overall level of its trade-distorting support from bound levels.

- As well as this overall commitment, Final Bound Total AMS and permitted *de minimis* levels will be subject to substantial reductions and, in the case of the Blue Box, will be capped as specified in paragraph 15 in order to ensure results that are coherent with the long-term reform objective. Any clarification or development of rules and conditions to govern trade distorting support will take this into account.

Overall Reduction: A Tiered Formula

7.   The overall base level of all trade-distorting domestic support, as measured by the Final Bound Total AMS plus permitted *de minimis* level and the level agreed in paragraph 8 below for Blue Box payments, will be reduced according to a tiered formula. Under this formula, Members having higher levels of trade-distorting domestic support will make greater overall reductions in order to achieve a harmonizing result. As the first instalment of the overall cut, in the first year and throughout the implementation period, the sum of all trade-distorting support will not exceed 80 per cent of the sum of Final Bound Total AMS plus permitted *de minimis* plus the Blue Box at the level determined in paragraph 15.

8.   The following parameters will guide the further negotiation of this tiered formula:

- This commitment will apply as a minimum overall commitment. It will not be applied as a ceiling on reductions of overall trade-distorting domestic support, should the separate and complementary formulae to be developed for Total AMS, *de minimis* and Blue Box payments imply, when taken together, a deeper cut in overall trade-distorting domestic support for an individual Member.

- The base for measuring the Blue Box component will be the higher of existing Blue Box payments during a recent representative period to be agreed and the cap established in paragraph 15 below.

Final Bound Total AMS: A Tiered Formula

9.   To achieve reductions with a harmonizing effect:

- Final Bound Total AMS will be reduced substantially, using a tiered approach.

- Members having higher Total AMS will make greater reductions.

- To prevent circumvention of the objective of the Agreement through transfers of unchanged domestic support between different support categories, product-specific AMSs will be capped at their respective average levels according to a methodology to be agreed.

- Substantial reductions in Final Bound Total AMS will result in reductions of some product-specific support.

10.   Members may make greater than formula reductions in order to achieve the required level of cut in overall trade-distorting domestic support.

De Minimis

11.   Reductions in *de minimis* will be negotiated taking into account the principle of special and differential treatment. Developing countries that allocate almost all *de minimis* support for subsistence and resource-poor farmers will be exempt.

12.   Members may make greater than formula reductions in order to achieve the required level of cut in overall trade-distorting domestic support.

Blue Box

13.   Members recognize the role of the Blue Box in promoting agricultural reforms. In this light, Article 6.5 will be reviewed so that Members may have recourse to the following measures:

- Direct payments under production-limiting programmes if:
    – such payments are based on fixed and unchanging areas and yields; or

    – such payments are made on 85% or less of a fixed and unchanging base level of production; or

    – livestock payments are made on a fixed and unchanging number of head.

Or

- Direct payments that do not require production if:
    – such payments are based on fixed and unchanging bases and yields; or

    – livestock payments made on a fixed and unchanging number of head; and

    – such payments are made on 85% or less of a fixed and unchanging base level of production.

14.   The above criteria, along with additional criteria will be negotiated. Any such criteria will ensure that Blue Box payments are less trade-distorting than AMS measures, it being understood that:

- Any new criteria would need to take account of the balance of WTO rights and obligations.

- Any new criteria to be agreed will not have the perverse effect of undoing ongoing reforms.

15.   Blue Box support will not exceed 5% of a Member's average total value of agricultural production during an historical period. The historical period will be established in the negotiations. This ceiling will apply to any actual or potential Blue Box user from the beginning of the implementation period. In cases where a Member has placed an exceptionally large percentage of its trade-distorting support in the Blue Box, some flexibility will be provided on a basis to be agreed to ensure that such a Member is not called upon to make a wholly disproportionate cut.

Green Box

16.   Green Box criteria will be reviewed and clarified with a view to ensuring that Green Box measures have no, or at most minimal, trade-distorting effects or effects on production. Such a review and clarification will need to ensure that the basic concepts, principles and effectiveness of the Green Box remain and take due account of non-trade concerns. The improved obligations for monitoring and surveillance of all new disciplines foreshadowed in paragraph 48 below will be particularly important with respect to the Green Box.

EXPORT COMPETITION

17.   The Doha Ministerial Declaration calls for "reduction of, with a view to phasing out, all forms of export subsidies". As an outcome of the negotiations, Members agree to establish detailed modalities ensuring the parallel elimination of all forms of export subsidies and disciplines on all export measures with equivalent effect by a credible end date.

End Point

18.   The following will be eliminated by the end date to be agreed:

- Export subsidies as scheduled.

- Export credits, export credit guarantees or insurance programmes with repayment periods beyond 180 days.

- Terms and conditions relating to export credits, export credit guarantees or insurance programmes with repayment periods of 180 days and below which are not in accordance with disciplines to be agreed. These disciplines will cover, *inter alia*, payment of interest, minimum interest rates, minimum premium requirements, and other elements which can constitute subsidies or otherwise distort trade.

- Trade distorting practices with respect to exporting STEs including eliminating export subsidies provided to or by them, government financing, and the underwriting of losses. The issue of the future use of monopoly powers will be subject to further negotiation.

- Provision of food aid that is not in conformity with operationally effective disciplines to be agreed. The objective of such disciplines will be to prevent commercial displacement. The role of international organizations as regards the provision of food aid by Members, including related humanitarian and developmental issues, will be addressed in the negotiations. The question of providing food aid exclusively in fully grant form will also be addressed in the negotiations.

19.   Effective transparency provisions for paragraph 18 will be established. Such provisions, in accordance with standard WTO practice, will be consistent with commercial confidentiality considerations.

Implementation

20.   Commitments and disciplines in paragraph 18 will be implemented according to a schedule and modalities to be agreed. Commitments will be implemented by annual instalments. Their phasing will take into account the need for some coherence with internal reform steps of Members.

21.   The negotiation of the elements in paragraph 18 and their implementation will ensure equivalent and parallel commitments by Members.

Special and Differential Treatment

22.   Developing country Members will benefit from longer implementation periods for the phasing out of all forms of export subsidies.

23.   Developing countries will continue to benefit from special and differential treatment under the provisions of Article 9.4 of the Agreement on Agriculture for a reasonable period, to be negotiated, after the phasing out of all forms of export subsidies and implementation of all disciplines identified above are completed.

24.   Members will ensure that the disciplines on export credits, export credit guarantees or insurance programs to be agreed will make appropriate provision for differential treatment in favour of least-developed and net food-importing developing countries as provided for in paragraph 4 of the Decision on Measures Concerning the Possible Negative Effects of the Reform Programme on Least-Developed and Net Food-Importing Developing Countries. Improved obligations for monitoring and surveillance of all new disciplines as foreshadowed in paragraph 48 will be critically important in this regard. Provisions to be agreed in this respect must not undermine the commitments undertaken by Members under the obligations in paragraph 18 above.

25.   STEs in developing country Members which enjoy special privileges to preserve domestic consumer price stability and to ensure food security will receive special consideration for maintaining monopoly status.

Special Circumstances

26.   In exceptional circumstances, which cannot be adequately covered by food aid, commercial export credits or preferential international financing facilities, ad hoc temporary financing arrangements relating to exports to developing countries may be agreed by Members. Such agreements must not have the effect of undermining commitments undertaken by Members in paragraph 18 above, and will be based on criteria and consultation procedures to be established.

MARKET ACCESS

27.   The Doha Ministerial Declaration calls for "substantial improvements in market access". Members also agreed that special and differential treatment for developing Members would be an integral part of all elements in the negotiations.

The Single Approach: a Tiered Formula

28.   To ensure that a single approach for developed and developing country Members meets all the objectives of the Doha mandate, tariff reductions will be made through a tiered formula that takes into account their different tariff structures.

29.   To ensure that such a formula will lead to substantial trade expansion, the following principles will guide its further negotiation:

- Tariff reductions will be made from bound rates. Substantial overall tariff reductions will be achieved as a final result from negotiations.

- Each Member (other than LDCs) will make a contribution. Operationally effective special and differential provisions for developing country Members will be an integral part of all elements.

- Progressivity in tariff reductions will be achieved through deeper cuts in higher tariffs with flexibilities for sensitive products. Substantial improvements in market access will be achieved for all products.

30. The number of bands, the thresholds for defining the bands and the type of tariff reduction in each band remain under negotiation. The role of a tariff cap in a tiered formula with distinct treatment for sensitive products will be further evaluated.

Sensitive Products

Selection

31. Without undermining the overall objective of the tiered approach, Members may designate an appropriate number, to be negotiated, of tariff lines to be treated as sensitive, taking account of existing commitments for these products.

Treatment

32. The principle of 'substantial improvement' will apply to each product.

33. 'Substantial improvement' will be achieved through combinations of tariff quota commitments and tariff reductions applying to each product. However, balance in this negotiation will be found only if the final negotiated result also reflects the sensitivity of the product concerned.

34. Some MFN-based tariff quota expansion will be required for all such products. A base for such an expansion will be established, taking account of coherent and equitable criteria to be developed in the negotiations. In order not to undermine the objective of the tiered approach, for all such products, MFN based tariff quota expansion will be provided under specific rules to be negotiated taking into account deviations from the tariff formula.

Other Elements

35. Other elements that will give the flexibility required to reach a final balanced result include reduction or elimination of in-quota tariff rates, and operationally effective improvements in tariff quota administration for existing tariff quotas so as to enable Members, and particularly developing country Members, to fully benefit from the market access opportunities under tariff rate quotas.

36. Tariff escalation will be addressed through a formula to be agreed.

37. The issue of tariff simplification remains under negotiation.

38. The question of the special agricultural safeguard (SSG) remains under negotiation.

Special and differential treatment

39.   Having regard to their rural development, food security and/or livelihood security needs, special and differential treatment for developing countries will be an integral part of all elements of the negotiation, including the tariff reduction formula, the number and treatment of sensitive products, expansion of tariff rate quotas, and implementation period.

40.   Proportionality will be achieved by requiring lesser tariff reduction commitments or tariff quota expansion commitments from developing country Members.

41.   Developing country Members will have the flexibility to designate an appropriate number of products as Special Products, based on criteria of food security, livelihood security and rural development needs. These products will be eligible for more flexible treatment. The criteria and treatment of these products will be further specified during the negotiation phase and will recognize the fundamental importance of Special Products to developing countries.

42.   A Special Safeguard Mechanism (SSM) will be established for use by developing country Members.

43.   Full implementation of the long-standing commitment to achieve the fullest liberalisation of trade in tropical agricultural products and for products of particular importance to the diversification of production from the growing of illicit narcotic crops is overdue and will be addressed effectively in the market access negotiations.

44.   The importance of long-standing preferences is fully recognised. The issue of preference erosion will be addressed. For the further consideration in this regard, paragraph 16 and other relevant provisions of TN/AG/W/1/Rev.1 will be used as a reference.

LEAST- DEVELOPED COUNTRIES

45.   Least-Developed Countries, which will have full access to all special and differential treatment provisions above, are not required to undertake reduction commitments. Developed Members, and developing country Members in a position to do so, should provide duty-free and quota-free market access for products originating from least-developed countries.

46.   Work on cotton under all the pillars will reflect the vital importance of this sector to certain LDC Members and we will work to achieve ambitious results expeditiously.

RECENTLY ACCEDED MEMBERS

47.   The particular concerns of recently acceded Members will be effectively addressed through specific flexibility provisions.

MONITORING AND SURVEILLANCE

48.   Article 18 of the Agreement on Agriculture will be amended with a view to enhancing monitoring so as to effectively ensure full transparency, including through timely and complete notifications with respect to the commitments in market access, domestic support and export competition. The particular concerns of developing countries in this regard will be addressed.

OTHER ISSUES

49.   Issues of interest but not agreed: sectoral initiatives, differential export taxes, GIs.

50.   Disciplines on export prohibitions and restrictions in Article 12.1 of the Agreement on Agriculture will be strengthened.

Annex B

Framework for Establishing Modalities in
Market Access for Non-Agricultural Products

1.   This Framework contains the initial elements for future work on modalities by the Negotiating Group on Market Access. Additional negotiations are required to reach agreement on the specifics of some of these elements. These relate to the formula, the issues concerning the treatment of unbound tariffs in indent two of paragraph 5, the flexibilities for developing-country participants, the issue of participation in the sectoral tariff component and the preferences. In order to finalize the modalities, the Negotiating Group is instructed to address these issues expeditiously in a manner consistent with the mandate of paragraph 16 of the Doha Ministerial Declaration and the overall balance therein.

2.   We reaffirm that negotiations on market access for non-agricultural products shall aim to reduce or as appropriate eliminate tariffs, including the reduction or elimination of tariff peaks, high tariffs, and tariff escalation, as well as non-tariff barriers, in particular on products of export interest to developing countries. We also reaffirm the importance of special and differential treatment and less than full reciprocity in reduction commitments as integral parts of the modalities.

3.   We acknowledge the substantial work undertaken by the Negotiating Group on Market Access and the progress towards achieving an agreement on negotiating modalities. We take note of the constructive dialogue on the Chair's Draft Elements of Modalities (TN/MA/W/35/Rev.1) and confirm our intention to use this document as a reference for the future work of the Negotiating Group. We instruct the Negotiating Group to continue its work, as mandated by paragraph 16 of the Doha Ministerial Declaration with its corresponding references to the relevant provisions of Article XXVIII *bis* of GATT 1994 and to the provisions cited in paragraph 50 of the Doha Ministerial Declaration, on the basis set out below.

4.   We recognize that a formula approach is key to reducing tariffs, and reducing or eliminating tariff peaks, high tariffs, and tariff escalation. We agree that the Negotiating Group should continue its work on a non-linear formula applied on a line-by-line basis which shall take fully into account the special needs and interests of developing and least-developed country participants, including through less than full reciprocity in reduction commitments.

5.   We further agree on the following elements regarding the formula:

–   product coverage shall be comprehensive without *a priori* exclusions;

- tariff reductions or elimination shall commence from the bound rates after full implementation of current concessions; however, for unbound tariff lines, the basis for commencing the tariff reductions shall be [two] times the MFN applied rate in the base year;

- the base year for MFN applied tariff rates shall be 2001 (applicable rates on 14 November);

- credit shall be given for autonomous liberalization by developing countries provided that the tariff lines were bound on an MFN basis in the WTO since the conclusion of the Uruguay Round;

- all non-*ad valorem* duties shall be converted to *ad valorem* equivalents on the basis of a methodology to be determined and bound in *ad valorem* terms;

- negotiations shall commence on the basis of the HS96 or HS2002 nomenclature, with the results of the negotiations to be finalized in HS2002 nomenclature;

- the reference period for import data shall be 1999–2001.

6.　　We furthermore agree that, as an exception, participants with a binding coverage of non-agricultural tariff lines of less than [35] percent would be exempt from making tariff reductions through the formula. Instead, we expect them to bind [100] percent of non-agricultural tariff lines at an average level that does not exceed the overall average of bound tariffs for all developing countries after full implementation of current concessions.

7.　　We recognize that a sectorial tariff component, aiming at elimination or harmonization is another key element to achieving the objectives of paragraph 16 of the Doha Ministerial Declaration with regard to the reduction or elimination of tariffs, in particular on products of export interest to developing countries. We recognize that participation by all participants will be important to that effect. We therefore instruct the Negotiating Group to pursue its discussions on such a component, with a view to defining product coverage, participation, and adequate provisions of flexibility for developing-country participants.

8.　　We agree that developing-country participants shall have longer implementation periods for tariff reductions. In addition, they shall be given the following flexibility:

a) applying less than formula cuts to up to [10] percent of the tariff lines provided that the cuts are no less than half the formula cuts and that these tariff lines do not exceed [10] percent of the total value of a Member's imports; or

b) keeping, as an exception, tariff lines unbound, or not applying formula cuts for up to [5] percent of tariff lines provided they do not exceed [5] percent of the total value of a Member's imports.

We furthermore agree that this flexibility could not be used to exclude entire HS Chapters.

9. We agree that least-developed country participants shall not be required to apply the formula nor participate in the sectorial approach, however, as part of their contribution to this round of negotiations, they are expected to substantially increase their level of binding commitments.

10. Furthermore, in recognition of the need to enhance the integration of least-developed countries into the multilateral trading system and support the diversification of their production and export base, we call upon developed-country participants and other participants who so decide, to grant on an autonomous basis duty-free and quota-free market access for non-agricultural products originating from least-developed countries by the year [...].

11. We recognize that newly acceded Members shall have recourse to special provisions for tariff reductions in order to take into account their extensive market access commitments undertaken as part of their accession and that staged tariff reductions are still being implemented in many cases. We instruct the Negotiating Group to further elaborate on such provisions.

12. We agree that pending agreement on core modalities for tariffs, the possibilities of supplementary modalities such as zero-for-zero sector elimination, sectorial harmonization, and request & offer, should be kept open.

13. In addition, we ask developed-country participants and other participants who so decide to consider the elimination of low duties.

14. We recognize that NTBs are an integral and equally important part of these negotiations and instruct participants to intensify their work on NTBs. In particular, we encourage all participants to make notifications on NTBs by 31 October 2004 and to proceed with identification, examination, categorization, and ultimately negotiations on NTBs. We take note that the modalities for addressing NTBs in these negotiations could include request/

offer, horizontal, or vertical approaches; and should fully take into account the principle of special and differential treatment for developing and least-developed country participants.

15.   We recognize that appropriate studies and capacity building measures shall be an integral part of the modalities to be agreed. We also recognize the work that has already been undertaken in these areas and ask participants to continue to identify such issues to improve participation in the negotiations.

16.   We recognize the challenges that may be faced by non-reciprocal preference beneficiary Members and those Members that are at present highly dependent on tariff revenue as a result of these negotiations on non-agricultural products. We instruct the Negotiating Group to take into consideration, in the course of its work, the particular needs that may arise for the Members concerned.

17.   We furthermore encourage the Negotiating Group to work closely with the Committee on Trade and Environment in Special Session with a view to addressing the issue of non-agricultural environmental goods covered in paragraph 31 (iii) of the Doha Ministerial Declaration.

Annex C

Recommendations of the Special Session of the Council for Trade in Services

(a)   Members who have not yet submitted their initial offers must do so as soon as possible.

(b)   A date for the submission of a round of revised offers should be established as soon as feasible.

(c)   With a view to providing effective market access to all Members and in order to ensure a substantive outcome, Members shall strive to ensure a high quality of offers, particularly in sectors and modes of supply of export interest to developing countries, with special attention to be given to least-developed countries.

(d)   Members shall aim to achieve progressively higher levels of liberalization with no a priori exclusion of any service sector or mode of supply and shall give special attention to sectors and modes of supply of export interest to developing countries. Members note the interest of developing countries, as well as other Members, in Mode 4.

(e)   Members must intensify their efforts to conclude the negotiations on rule-making under GATS Articles VI:4, X, XIII and XV in accordance with their respective mandates and deadlines.

(f)   Targeted technical assistance should be provided with a view to enabling developing countries to participate effectively in the negotiations.

(g)   For the purpose of the Sixth Ministerial meeting, the Special Session of the Council for Trade in Services shall review progress in these negotiations and provide a full report to the Trade Negotiations Committee, including possible recommendations.

Annex D

Modalities for Negotiations on Trade Facilitation

1.   Negotiations shall aim to clarify and improve relevant aspects of Articles V, VIII and X of the GATT 1994 with a view to further expediting the movement, release and clearance of goods, including goods in transit.[1] Negotiations shall also aim at enhancing technical assistance and support for capacity building in this area. The negotiations shall further aim at provisions for effective cooperation between customs or any other appropriate authorities on trade facilitation and customs compliance issues.

2.   The results of the negotiations shall take fully into account the principle of special and differential treatment for developing and least-developed countries. Members recognize that this principle should extend beyond the granting of traditional transition periods for implementing commitments. In particular, the extent and the timing of entering into commitments shall be related to the implementation capacities of developing and least-developed Members. It is further agreed that those Members would not be obliged to undertake investments in infrastructure projects beyond their means.

3.   Least-developed country Members will only be required to undertake commitments to the extent consistent with their individual development, financial and trade needs or their administrative and institutional capabilities.

4.   As an integral part of the negotiations, Members shall seek to identify their trade facilitation needs and priorities, particularly those of developing and least-developed countries, and shall also address the concerns of developing and least-developed countries related to cost implications of proposed measures.

5.   It is recognized that the provision of technical assistance and support for capacity building is vital for developing and least-developed countries to enable them to fully participate in and benefit from the negotiations. Members, in particular developed countries, therefore commit themselves to adequately ensure such support and assistance during the negotiations.[2]

6.   Support and assistance should also be provided to help developing and least-developed countries implement the commitments resulting from the negotiations, in accordance with their nature and scope. In this context, it is recognized that negotiations could lead to certain commitments whose implementation would require support for infrastructure development on the part of some Members. In these limited cases, developed-country

Members will make every effort to ensure support and assistance directly related to the nature and scope of the commitments in order to allow implementation. It is understood, however, that in cases where required support and assistance for such infrastructure is not forthcoming, and where a developing or least-developed Member continues to lack the necessary capacity, implementation will not be required. While every effort will be made to ensure the necessary support and assistance, it is understood that the commitments by developed countries to provide such support are not open-ended.

7.   Members agree to review the effectiveness of the support and assistance provided and its ability to support the implementation of the results of the negotiations.

8.   In order to make technical assistance and capacity building more effective and operational and to ensure better coherence, Members shall invite relevant international organizations, including the IMF, OECD, UNCTAD, WCO and the World Bank to undertake a collaborative effort in this regard.

9.   Due account shall be taken of the relevant work of the WCO and other relevant international organizations in this area.

10.   Paragraphs 45-51 of the Doha Ministerial Declaration shall apply to these negotiations. At its first meeting after the July session of the General Council, the Trade Negotiations Committee shall establish a Negotiating Group on Trade Facilitation and appoint its Chair. The first meeting of the Negotiating Group shall agree on a work plan and schedule of meetings.

Notes

[1]   It is understood that this is without prejudice to the possible format of the final result of the negotiations and would allow consideration of various forms of outcomes.

[2]   In connection with this paragraph, Members note that paragraph 38 of the Doha Ministerial Declaration addresses relevant technical assistance and capacity building concerns of Members.

Hong Kong Ministerial Conference Declaration

WT/MIN(05)/DEC
22 December 2005
(05-6248)

MINISTERIAL CONFERENCE
Sixth Session
Hong Kong, 13–18 December 2005

DOHA WORK PROGRAMME
Ministerial Declaration
Adopted on 18 December 2005

1.   We reaffirm the Declarations and Decisions we adopted at Doha, as well as the Decision adopted by the General Council on 1 August 2004, and our full commitment to give effect to them. We renew our resolve to complete the Doha Work Programme fully and to conclude the negotiations launched at Doha successfully in 2006.

2.   We emphasize the central importance of the development dimension in every aspect of the Doha Work Programme and recommit ourselves to making it a meaningful reality, in terms both of the results of the negotiations on market access and rule-making and of the specific development-related issues set out below.

3.   In pursuance of these objectives, we agree as follows:

Agriculture negotiations   4.   We reaffirm our commitment to the mandate on agriculture as set out in paragraph 13 of the Doha Ministerial Declaration and to the Framework adopted by the General Council on 1 August 2004. We take note of the report by the Chairman of the Special Session on his own responsibility (TN/AG/21, contained in Annex A). We welcome the progress made by the Special Session of the Committee on Agriculture since 2004 and recorded therein.

5.   On domestic support, there will be three bands for reductions in Final Bound Total AMS and in the overall cut in trade-distorting domestic support, with higher linear cuts in higher bands. In both cases, the Member with the highest level of permitted support will be in the top band, the two Members with the second and third highest levels of

101

support will be in the middle band and all other Members, including all developing country Members, will be in the bottom band. In addition, developed country Members in the lower bands with high relative levels of Final Bound Total AMS will make an additional effort in AMS reduction. We also note that there has been some convergence concerning the reductions in Final Bound Total AMS, the overall cut in trade-distorting domestic support and in both product-specific and non product-specific *de minimis* limits. Disciplines will be developed to achieve effective cuts in trade-distorting domestic support consistent with the Framework. The overall reduction in trade-distorting domestic support will still need to be made even if the sum of the reductions in Final Bound Total AMS, *de minimis* and Blue Box payments would otherwise be less than that overall reduction. Developing country Members with no AMS commitments will be exempt from reductions in *de minimis* and the overall cut in trade-distorting domestic support. Green Box criteria will be reviewed in line with paragraph 16 of the Framework, *inter alia*, to ensure that programmes of developing country Members that cause not more than minimal trade-distortion are effectively covered.

6.   We agree to ensure the parallel elimination of all forms of export subsidies and disciplines on all export measures with equivalent effect to be completed by the end of 2013. This will be achieved in a progressive and parallel manner, to be specified in the modalities, so that a substantial part is realized by the end of the first half of the implementation period. We note emerging convergence on some elements of disciplines with respect to export credits, export credit guarantees or insurance programmes with repayment periods of 180 days and below. We agree that such programmes should be self-financing, reflecting market consistency, and that the period should be of a sufficiently short duration so as not to effectively circumvent real commercially-oriented discipline. As a means of ensuring that trade-distorting practices of STEs are eliminated, disciplines relating to exporting STEs will extend to the future use of monopoly powers so that such powers cannot be exercised in any way that would circumvent the direct disciplines on STEs on export subsidies, government financing and the underwriting of losses. On food aid, we reconfirm our commitment to maintain an adequate level and to

take into account the interests of food aid recipient countries. To this end, a "safe box" for bona fide food aid will be provided to ensure that there is no unintended impediment to dealing with emergency situations. Beyond that, we will ensure elimination of commercial displacement. To this end, we will agree effective disciplines on in-kind food aid, monetization and re-exports so that there can be no loop-hole for continuing export subsidization. The disciplines on export credits, export credit guarantees or insurance programmes, exporting state trading enterprises and food aid will be completed by 30 April 2006 as part of the modalities, including appropriate provision in favour of least-developed and net food-importing developing countries as provided for in paragraph 4 of the Marrakesh Decision. The date above for the elimination of all forms of export subsidies, together with the agreed progressivity and parallelism, will be confirmed only upon the completion of the modalities. Developing country Members will continue to benefit from the provisions of Article 9.4 of the Agreement on Agriculture for five years after the end-date for elimination of all forms of export subsidies.

7.　　On market access, we note the progress made on *ad valorem* equivalents. We adopt four bands for structuring tariff cuts, recognizing that we need now to agree on the relevant thresholds - including those applicable for developing country Members. We recognize the need to agree on treatment of sensitive products, taking into account all the elements involved. We also note that there have been some recent movements on the designation and treatment of Special Products and elements of the Special Safeguard Mechanism. Developing country Members will have the flexibility to self-designate an appropriate number of tariff lines as Special Products guided by indicators based on the criteria of food security, livelihood security and rural development. Developing country Members will also have the right to have recourse to a Special Safeguard Mechanism based on import quantity and price triggers, with precise arrangements to be further defined. Special Products and the Special Safeguard Mechanism shall be an integral part of the modalities and the outcome of negotiations in agriculture.

8.　　On other elements of special and differential treatment, we note in particular the consensus that exists in the Framework on several issues in all three pillars of domestic support, export competition and market access and that some progress has been made on other special and differential treatment issues.

9.   We reaffirm that nothing we have agreed here compromises the agreement already reflected in the Framework on other issues including tropical products and products of particular importance to the diversification of production from the growing of illicit narcotic crops, long-standing preferences and preference erosion.

10.   However, we recognize that much remains to be done in order to establish modalities and to conclude the negotiations. Therefore, we agree to intensify work on all outstanding issues to fulfil the Doha objectives, in particular, we are resolved to establish modalities no later than 30 April 2006 and to submit comprehensive draft Schedules based on these modalities no later than 31 July 2006.

Cotton   11.   We recall the mandate given by the Members in the Decision adopted by the General Council on 1 August 2004 to address cotton ambitiously, expeditiously and specifically, within the agriculture negotiations in relation to all trade-distorting policies affecting the sector in all three pillars of market access, domestic support and export competition, as specified in the Doha text and the July 2004 Framework text. We note the work already undertaken in the Sub-Committee on Cotton and the proposals made with regard to this matter. Without prejudice to Members' current WTO rights and obligations, including those flowing from actions taken by the Dispute Settlement Body, we reaffirm our commitment to ensure having an explicit decision on cotton within the agriculture negotiations and through the Sub-Committee on Cotton ambitiously, expeditiously and specifically as follows:

–   All forms of export subsidies for cotton will be eliminated by developed countries in 2006.

–   On market access, developed countries will give duty and quota free access for cotton exports from least-developed countries (LDCs) from the commencement of the implementation period.

–   Members agree that the objective is that, as an outcome for the negotiations, trade distorting domestic subsidies for cotton production be reduced more ambitiously than under whatever general formula is agreed and that it should be implemented over a shorter period of time than generally applicable. We commit ourselves to give priority in the negotiations to reach such an outcome.

12.   With regard to the development assistance aspects of cotton, we welcome the Consultative Framework process initiated by the Director-General to implement the decisions on these aspects pursuant to paragraph 1.b of the Decision adopted by the General Council on 1 August 2004. We take note of his Periodic Reports and the positive evolution of development assistance noted therein. We urge the Director-General to further intensify his consultative efforts with bilateral donors and with multilateral and regional institutions, with emphasis on improved coherence, coordination and enhanced implementation and to explore the possibility of establishing through such institutions a mechanism to deal with income declines in the cotton sector until the end of subsidies. Noting the importance of achieving enhanced efficiency and competitiveness in the cotton producing process, we urge the development community to further scale up its cotton-specific assistance and to support the efforts of the Director-General. In this context, we urge Members to promote and support South-South cooperation, including transfer of technology. We welcome the domestic reform efforts by African cotton producers aimed at enhancing productivity and efficiency, and encourage them to deepen this process. We reaffirm the complementarity of the trade policy and development assistance aspects of cotton. We invite the Director-General to furnish a third Periodic Report to our next Session with updates, at appropriate intervals in the meantime, to the General Council, while keeping the Sub-Committee on Cotton fully informed of progress. Finally, as regards follow up and monitoring, we request the Director-General to set up an appropriate follow-up and monitoring mechanism.

NAMA negotiations   13.   We reaffirm our commitment to the mandate for negotiations on market access for non-agricultural products as set out in paragraph 16 of the Doha Ministerial Declaration. We also reaffirm all the elements of the

NAMA Framework adopted by the General Council on 1 August 2004. We take note of the report by the Chairman of the Negotiating Group on Market Access on his own responsibility (TN/MA/16, contained in Annex B). We welcome the progress made by the Negotiating Group on Market Access since 2004 and recorded therein.

14.   We adopt a Swiss Formula with coefficients at levels which shall *inter alia*:

–   Reduce or as appropriate eliminate tariffs, including the reduction or elimination of tariff peaks, high tariffs and tariff escalation, in particular on products of export interest to developing countries; and

–   Take fully into account the special needs and interests of developing countries, including through less than full reciprocity in reduction commitments.

We instruct the Negotiating Group to finalize its structure and details as soon as possible.

15.   We reaffirm the importance of special and differential treatment and less than full reciprocity in reduction commitments, including paragraph 8 of the NAMA Framework, as integral parts of the modalities. We instruct the Negotiating Group to finalize its details as soon as possible.

16.   In furtherance of paragraph 7 of the NAMA Framework, we recognize that Members are pursuing sectoral initiatives. To this end, we instruct the Negotiating Group to review proposals with a view to identifying those which could garner sufficient participation to be realized. Participation should be on a non-mandatory basis.

17.   For the purpose of the second indent of paragraph 5 of the NAMA Framework, we adopt a non-linear mark-up approach to establish base rates for commencing tariff reductions. We instruct the Negotiating Group to finalize its details as soon as possible.

18.   We take note of the progress made to convert non *ad valorem* duties to *ad valorem* equivalents on the basis of an agreed methodology as contained in JOB(05)/166/Rev.1.

19.   We take note of the level of common understanding reached on the issue of product coverage and direct the Negotiating Group to resolve differences on the limited issues that remain as quickly as possible.

20.   As a supplement to paragraph 16 of the NAMA Framework, we recognize the challenges that may be faced by non-reciprocal preference beneficiary Members as a consequence of the MFN liberalization that will result from these negotiations. We instruct the Negotiating Group to intensify work on the assessment of the scope of the problem with a view to finding possible solutions.

21.   We note the concerns raised by small, vulnerable economies, and instruct the Negotiating Group to establish ways to provide flexibilities for these Members without creating a sub-category of WTO Members.

22.   We note that the Negotiating Group has made progress in the identification, categorization and examination of notified NTBs. We also take note that Members are developing bilateral, vertical and horizontal approaches to the NTB negotiations, and that some of the NTBs are being addressed in other fora including other Negotiating Groups. We recognize the need for specific negotiating proposals and encourage participants to make such submissions as quickly as possible.

23.   However, we recognize that much remains to be done in order to establish modalities and to conclude the negotiations. Therefore, we agree to intensify work on all outstanding issues to fulfil the Doha objectives, in particular, we are resolved to establish modalities no later than 30 April 2006 and to submit comprehensive draft Schedules based on these modalities no later than 31 July 2006.

Balance between Agriculture and NAMA   24.   We recognize that it is important to advance the development objectives of this Round through enhanced market access for developing countries in both Agriculture and NAMA. To that end, we instruct our negotiators to ensure that there is a comparably high level of ambition in market access for Agriculture and NAMA. This ambition is to be achieved in a balanced and proportionate manner consistent with the principle of special and differential treatment.

Services
negotiations

25.   The negotiations on trade in services shall proceed to their conclusion with a view to promoting the economic growth of all trading partners and the development of developing and least-developed countries, and with due respect for the right of Members to regulate. In this regard, we recall and reaffirm the objectives and principles stipulated in the GATS, the Doha Ministerial Declaration, the Guidelines and Procedures for the Negotiations on Trade in Services adopted by the Special Session of the Council for Trade in Services on 28 March 2001 and the Modalities for the Special Treatment for Least-Developed Country Members in the Negotiations on Trade in Services adopted on 3 September 2003, as well as Annex C of the Decision adopted by the General Council on 1 August 2004.

26.   We urge all Members to participate actively in these negotiations towards achieving a progressively higher level of liberalization of trade in services, with appropriate flexibility for individual developing countries as provided for in Article XIX of the GATS. Negotiations shall have regard to the size of economies of individual Members, both overall and in individual sectors. We recognize the particular economic situation of LDCs, including the difficulties they face, and acknowledge that they are not expected to undertake new commitments.

27.   We are determined to intensify the negotiations in accordance with the above principles and the Objectives, Approaches and Timelines set out in Annex C to this document with a view to expanding the sectoral and modal coverage of commitments and improving their quality. In this regard, particular attention will be given to sectors and modes of supply of export interest to developing countries.

Rules
negotiations

28.   We recall the mandates in paragraphs 28 and 29 of the Doha Ministerial Declaration and reaffirm our commitment to the negotiations on rules, as we set forth in Annex D to this document.

TRIPS
negotiations

29.   We take note of the report of the Chairman of the Special Session of the Council for TRIPS setting out the progress in the negotiations on

the establishment of a multilateral system of notification and registration of geographical indications for wines and spirits, as mandated in Article 23.4 of the TRIPS Agreement and paragraph 18 of the Doha Ministerial Declaration, contained in document TN/IP/14, and agree to intensify these negotiations in order to complete them within the overall time-frame for the conclusion of the negotiations that were foreseen in the Doha Ministerial Declaration.

Environment negotiations   30.   We reaffirm the mandate in paragraph 31 of the Doha Ministerial Declaration aimed at enhancing the mutual supportiveness of trade and environment and welcome the significant work undertaken in the Committee on Trade and Environment (CTE) in Special Session. We instruct Members to intensify the negotiations, without prejudging their outcome, on all parts of paragraph 31 to fulfil the mandate.

31.   We recognize the progress in the work under paragraph 31(i) based on Members' submissions on the relationship between existing WTO rules and specific trade obligations set out in multilateral environmental agreements (MEAs). We further recognize the work undertaken under paragraph 31(ii) towards developing effective procedures for regular information exchange between MEA Secretariats and the relevant WTO committees, and criteria for the granting of observer status.

32.   We recognize that recently more work has been carried out under paragraph 31(iii) through numerous submissions by Members and discussions in the CTE in Special Session, including technical discussions, which were also held in informal information exchange sessions without prejudice to Members' positions. We instruct Members to complete the work expeditiously under paragraph 31(iii).

Trade Facilitation negotiations   33.   We recall and reaffirm the mandate and modalities for negotiations on Trade Facilitation contained in Annex D of the Decision adopted by the General Council on 1 August 2004. We note with appreciation the report of the Negotiating Group, attached in Annex E to this document, and the comments made by our delegations on that report as reflected in document TN/TF/M/11. We endorse the recommendations contained in paragraphs 3, 4, 5, 6 and 7 of the report.

DSU   34.   We take note of the progress made in the Dispute Settlement
negotiations Understanding negotiations as reflected in the report by the Chairman
               of the Special Session of the Dispute Settlement Body to the Trade
               Negotiations Committee (TNC) and direct the Special Session to
               continue to work towards a rapid conclusion of the negotiations.

S&D treatment 35.   We reaffirm that provisions for special and differential (S&D)
               treatment are an integral part of the WTO Agreements. We renew our
               determination to fulfil the mandate contained in paragraph 44 of the
               Doha Ministerial Declaration and in the Decision adopted by the General
               Council on 1 August 2004, that all S&D treatment provisions be reviewed
               with a view to strengthening them and making them more precise,
               effective and operational.

               36.   We take note of the work done on the Agreement-specific
               proposals, especially the five LDC proposals. We agree to adopt the
               decisions contained in Annex F to this document. However, we also
               recognize that substantial work still remains to be done. We commit
               ourselves to address the development interests and concerns of
               developing countries, especially the LDCs, in the multilateral trading
               system, and we recommit ourselves to complete the task we set
               ourselves at Doha. We accordingly instruct the Committee on Trade
               and Development in Special Session to expeditiously complete the
               review of all the outstanding Agreement-specific proposals and report
               to the General Council, with clear recommendations for a decision, by
               December 2006.

               37.   We are concerned at the lack of progress on the Category II
               proposals that had been referred to other WTO bodies and negotiating
               groups. We instruct these bodies to expeditiously complete the
               consideration of these proposals and report periodically to the General
               Council, with the objective of ensuring that clear recommendations for a
               decision are made no later than December 2006. We also instruct the
               Special Session to continue to coordinate its efforts with these bodies,
               so as to ensure that this work is completed on time.

               38.   We further instruct the Special Session, within the parameters
               of the Doha mandate, to resume work on all other outstanding issues,

including on the cross-cutting issues, the monitoring mechanism, and the incorporation of S&D treatment into the architecture of WTO rules, and report on a regular basis to the General Council.

Implementation   39.   We reiterate the instruction in the Decision adopted by the General Council on 1 August 2004 to the TNC, negotiating bodies and other WTO bodies concerned to redouble their efforts to find appropriate solutions as a priority to outstanding implementation-related issues. We take note of the work undertaken by the Director-General in his consultative process on all outstanding implementation issues under paragraph 12(b) of the Doha Ministerial Declaration, including on issues related to the extension of the protection of geographical indications provided for in Article 23 of the TRIPS Agreement to products other than wines and spirits and those related to the relationship between the TRIPS Agreement and the Convention on Biological Diversity. We request the Director-General, without prejudice to the positions of Members, to intensify his consultative process on all outstanding implementation issues under paragraph 12(b), if need be by appointing Chairpersons of concerned WTO bodies as his Friends and/or by holding dedicated consultations. The Director-General shall report to each regular meeting of the TNC and the General Council. The Council shall review progress and take any appropriate action no later than 31 July 2006.

TRIPS & Public   40.   We reaffirm the importance we attach to the General Council
Health   Decision of 30 August 2003 on the Implementation of Paragraph 6 of the Doha Declaration on the TRIPS Agreement and Public Health, and to an amendment to the TRIPS Agreement replacing its provisions. In this regard, we welcome the work that has taken place in the Council for TRIPS and the Decision of the General Council of 6 December 2005 on an Amendment of the TRIPS Agreement.

Small   41.   We reaffirm our commitment to the Work Programme on Small
Economies   Economies and urge Members to adopt specific measures that would facilitate the fuller integration of small, vulnerable economies into the multilateral trading system, without creating a sub-category of WTO Members. We take note of the report of the Committee on Trade and Development in Dedicated Session on the Work Programme on Small

Economies to the General Council and agree to the recommendations on future work. We instruct the Committee on Trade and Development, under the overall responsibility of the General Council, to continue the work in the Dedicated Session and to monitor progress of the small economies' proposals in the negotiating and other bodies, with the aim of providing responses to the trade-related issues of small economies as soon as possible but no later than 31 December 2006. We instruct the General Council to report on progress and action taken, together with any further recommendations as appropriate, to our next Session.

Trade, Debt & Finance

42.   We take note of the report transmitted by the General Council on the work undertaken and progress made in the examination of the relationship between trade, debt and finance and on the consideration of any possible recommendations on steps that might be taken within the mandate and competence of the WTO as provided in paragraph 36 of the Doha Ministerial Declaration and agree that, building on the work carried out to date, this work shall continue on the basis of the Doha mandate. We instruct the General Council to report further to our next Session.

Trade & Transfer of Technology

43.   We take note of the report transmitted by the General Council on the work undertaken and progress made in the examination of the relationship between trade and transfer of technology and on the consideration of any possible recommendations on steps that might be taken within the mandate of the WTO to increase flows of technology to developing countries. Recognizing the relevance of the relationship between trade and transfer of technology to the development dimension of the Doha Work Programme and building on the work carried out to date, we agree that this work shall continue on the basis of the mandate contained in paragraph 37 of the Doha Ministerial Declaration. We instruct the General Council to report further to our next Session.

Doha paragraph 19

44.   We take note of the work undertaken by the Council for TRIPS pursuant to paragraph 19 of the Doha Ministerial Declaration and agree that this work shall continue on the basis of paragraph 19 of the Doha Ministerial Declaration and the progress made in the Council for TRIPS to date. The General Council shall report on its work in this regard to our next Session.

TRIPS non-
violation and
situation
complaints

45.   We take note of the work done by the Council for Trade-Related Aspects of Intellectual Property Rights pursuant to paragraph 11.1 of the Doha Decision on Implementation-Related Issues and Concerns and paragraph 1.h of the Decision adopted by the General Council on 1 August 2004, and direct it to continue its examination of the scope and modalities for complaints of the types provided for under subparagraphs 1(b) and 1(c) of Article XXIII of GATT 1994 and make recommendations to our next Session. It is agreed that, in the meantime, Members will not initiate such complaints under the TRIPS Agreement.

E-commerce

46.   We take note of the reports from the General Council and subsidiary bodies on the Work Programme on Electronic Commerce, and that the examination of issues under the Work Programme is not yet complete. We agree to reinvigorate that work, including the development related issues under the Work Programme and discussions on the trade treatment, *inter alia*, of electronically delivered software. We agree to maintain the current institutional arrangements for the Work Programme. We declare that Members will maintain their current practice of not imposing customs duties on electronic transmissions until our next Session.

LDCs

47.   We reaffirm our commitment to effectively and meaningfully integrate LDCs into the multilateral trading system and shall continue to implement the WTO Work Programme for LDCs adopted in February 2002. We acknowledge the seriousness of the concerns and interests of the LDCs in the negotiations as expressed in the Livingstone Declaration, adopted by their Ministers in June 2005. We take note that issues of interest to LDCs are being addressed in all areas of negotiations and we welcome the progress made since the Doha Ministerial Declaration as reflected in the Decision adopted by the General Council on 1 August 2004. Building upon the commitment in the Doha Ministerial Declaration, developed-country Members, and developing-country Members declaring themselves in a position to do so, agree to implement duty-free and quota-free market access for products originating from LDCs as provided for in Annex F to this document. Furthermore, in accordance with our commitment in the Doha Ministerial Declaration, Members shall take additional measures to provide effective market

access, both at the border and otherwise, including simplified and transparent rules of origin so as to facilitate exports from LDCs. In the services negotiations, Members shall implement the LDC modalities and give priority to the sectors and modes of supply of export interest to LDCs, particularly with regard to movement of service providers under Mode 4. We agree to facilitate and accelerate negotiations with acceding LDCs based on the accession guidelines adopted by the General Council in December 2002. We commit to continue giving our attention and priority to concluding the ongoing accession proceedings as rapidly as possible. We welcome the Decision by the TRIPS Council to extend the transition period under Article 66.1 of the TRIPS Agreement. We reaffirm our commitment to enhance effective trade-related technical assistance and capacity building to LDCs on a priority basis in helping to overcome their limited human and institutional trade-related capacity to enable LDCs to maximize the benefits resulting from the Doha Development Agenda (DDA).

Integrated
Framework

48.   We continue to attach high priority to the effective implementation of the Integrated Framework (IF) and reiterate our endorsement of the IF as a viable instrument for LDCs' trade development, building on its principles of country ownership and partnership. We highlight the importance of contributing to reducing their supply side constraints. We reaffirm our commitment made at Doha, and recognize the urgent need to make the IF more effective and timely in addressing the trade-related development needs of LDCs.

49.   In this regard, we are encouraged by the endorsement by the Development Committee of the World Bank and International Monetary Fund (IMF) at its autumn 2005 meeting of an enhanced IF. We welcome the establishment of a Task Force by the Integrated Framework Working Group as endorsed by the IF Steering Committee (IFSC) as well as an agreement on the three elements which together constitute an enhanced IF. The Task Force, composed of donor and LDC members, will provide recommendations to the IFSC by April 2006. The enhanced IF shall enter into force no later than 31 December 2006.

50.   We agree that the Task Force, in line with its Mandate and based on the three elements agreed to, shall provide recommendations on how the implementation of the IF can be improved, *inter alia*, by considering ways to:

1.   provide increased, predictable, and additional funding on a multi-year basis;

2.   strengthen the IF in-country, including through mainstreaming trade into national development plans and poverty reduction strategies; more effective follow-up to diagnostic trade integration studies and implementation of action matrices; and achieving greater and more effective coordination amongst donors and IF stakeholders, including beneficiaries;

3.   improve the IF decision-making and management structure to ensure an effective and timely delivery of the increased financial resources and programmes.

51.   We welcome the increased commitment already expressed by some Members in the run-up to, and during, this Session. We urge other development partners to significantly increase their contribution to the IF Trust Fund. We also urge the six IF core agencies to continue to cooperate closely in the implementation of the IF, to increase their investments in this initiative and to intensify their assistance in trade-related infrastructure, private sector development and institution building to help LDCs expand and diversify their export base.

Technical   52.   We note with appreciation the substantial increase in trade-
Cooperation   related technical assistance since our Fourth Session, which reflects the enhanced commitment of Members to address the increased demand for technical assistance, through both bilateral and multilateral programmes. We note the progress made in the current approach to planning and implementation of WTO's programmes, as embodied in the Technical Assistance and Training Plans adopted by Members, as well as the improved quality of those programmes. We note that a strategic review of WTO's technical assistance is to be carried out by Members, and expect

that in future planning and implementation of training and technical assistance, the conclusions and recommendations of the review will be taken into account, as appropriate.

53.   We reaffirm the priorities established in paragraph 38 of the Doha Ministerial Declaration for the delivery of technical assistance and urge the Director-General to ensure that programmes focus accordingly on the needs of beneficiary countries and reflect the priorities and mandates adopted by Members. We endorse the application of appropriate needs assessment mechanisms and support the efforts to enhance ownership by beneficiaries, in order to ensure the sustainability of trade-related capacity building. We invite the Director-General to reinforce the partnerships and coordination with other agencies and regional bodies in the design and implementation of technical assistance programmes, so that all dimensions of trade-related capacity building are addressed, in a manner coherent with the programmes of other providers. In particular, we encourage all Members to cooperate with the International Trade Centre, which complements WTO work by providing a platform for business to interact with trade negotiators, and practical advice for small and medium-sized enterprises (SMEs) to benefit from the multilateral trading system. In this connection, we note the role of the Joint Integrated Technical Assistance Programme (JITAP) in building the capacity of participating countries.

54.   In order to continue progress in the effective and timely delivery of trade-related capacity building, in line with the priority Members attach to it, the relevant structures of the Secretariat should be strengthened and its resources enhanced. We reaffirm our commitment to ensure secure and adequate levels of funding for trade-related capacity building, including in the Doha Development Agenda Global Trust Fund, to conclude the Doha Work Programme and implement its results.

Commodity
Issues

55.   We recognize the dependence of several developing and least-developed countries on the export of commodities and the problems they face because of the adverse impact of the long-term decline and sharp fluctuation in the prices of these commodities. We take note of the work undertaken in the Committee on Trade and Development on commodity

issues, and instruct the Committee, within its mandate, to intensify its work in cooperation with other relevant international organizations and report regularly to the General Council with possible recommendations. We agree that the particular trade-related concerns of developing and least-developed countries related to commodities shall also be addressed in the course of the agriculture and NAMA negotiations. We further acknowledge that these countries may need support and technical assistance to overcome the particular problems they face, and urge Members and relevant international organizations to consider favourably requests by these countries for support and assistance.

Coherence   56.   We welcome the Director-General's actions to strengthen the WTO's cooperation with the IMF and the World Bank in the context of the WTO's Marrakesh mandate on Coherence, and invite him to continue to work closely with the General Council in this area. We value the General Council meetings that are held with the participation of the heads of the IMF and the World Bank to advance our Coherence mandate. We agree to continue building on that experience and expand the debate on international trade and development policymaking and inter-agency cooperation with the participation of relevant UN agencies. In that regard, we note the discussions taking place in the Working Group on Trade, Debt and Finance on, *inter alia*, the issue of Coherence, and look forward to any possible recommendations it may make on steps that might be taken within the mandate and competence of the WTO on this issue.

Aid for Trade   57.   We welcome the discussions of Finance and Development Ministers in various fora, including the Development Committee of the World Bank and IMF, that have taken place this year on expanding Aid for Trade. Aid for Trade should aim to help developing countries, particularly LDCs, to build the supply-side capacity and trade-related infrastructure that they need to assist them to implement and benefit from WTO Agreements and more broadly to expand their trade. Aid for Trade cannot be a substitute for the development benefits that will result from a successful conclusion to the DDA, particularly on market access. However, it can be a valuable complement to the DDA. We invite the Director-General to create a task force that shall provide recommendations on how to operationalize Aid for Trade. The Task Force will provide recommendations to the General Council by July 2006 on how Aid for Trade might contribute most effectively to the development dimension of the DDA. We also invite the Director-General to consult with Members as well as with the IMF and World Bank, relevant international organisations and the regional development banks with a view to reporting to the General Council on appropriate mechanisms to secure additional financial resources for Aid for Trade, where appropriate through grants and concessional loans.

Recently-
acceded
Members

58.   We recognize the special situation of recently-acceded Members who have undertaken extensive market access commitments at the time of accession. This situation will be taken into account in the negotiations.

Accessions

59.   We reaffirm our strong commitment to making the WTO truly global in scope and membership. We welcome those new Members who have completed their accession processes since our last Session, namely Nepal, Cambodia and Saudi Arabia. We note with satisfaction that Tonga has completed its accession negotiations to the WTO. These accessions further strengthen the rules-based multilateral trading system. We continue to attach priority to the 29 ongoing accessions with a view to concluding them as rapidly and smoothly as possible. We stress the importance of facilitating and accelerating the accession negotiations of least-developed countries, taking due account of the guidelines on LDC accession adopted by the General Council in December 2002.

Annex A

Agriculture
Report by the Chairman of the Special Session of the
Committee on Agriculture to the TNC

1.   The present report has been prepared on my own responsibility. I have done so in response to the direction of Members as expressed at the informal Special Session of the Committee on Agriculture on 11 November 2005. At that meeting, following the informal Heads of Delegation meeting the preceding day, Members made it crystal clear that they sought from me at this point an objective factual summary of where the negotiations have reached at this time. It was clear from that meeting that Members did not expect or desire anything that purported to be more than that. In particular, it was clear that, following the decision at the Heads of Delegation meeting that full modalities will not be achieved at Hong Kong, Members did not want anything that suggested implicit or explicit agreement where it did not exist.

2.   This is not, of course, the kind of paper that I would have chosen or preferred to have prepared at this point. Ideally, my task should have been to work with Members to generate a draft text of modalities. But this text reflects the reality of the present situation. There will be - because there must be if we are to conclude these negotiations - such a draft text in the future. I look at this now as a task postponed, but the precise timing of this is in the hands of Members.

3.   As for this paper, it is precisely what it is described to be. No more, no less. It is the Chairman's report and, as such, it goes from me to the TNC. It is not anything more than my personal report - in particular, it is not in any sense an agreed text of Members. It does not, therefore, in any way prejudge or prejudice the positions of Members on any matter within it or outside of it. And, it certainly does not bind Members in any way. It should go without saying that the agreed basis of our work is, and shall remain, the Doha Mandate itself and the Framework in the Decision adopted by the General Council on 1 August 2004.

4.   As to the character of the paper, I have endeavoured to reflect what I discerned as the wishes of Members when they directed me to prepare this paper. I have tried to capture as clearly as I can such conditional progress and convergence as has developed in the post-July 2004 period. In doing so, I have not tried to brush under the carpet divergences that remain, and the paper tries to be just as clear on those points. Of course, it is a summary report. As such, it cannot - and does not - recapitulate each and every detail on

each and every issue. But I took from Members' comments that they would prefer a paper which could 'orient' further discussion.

5. In that regard, I hope that anyone reading this paper would be able to get a pretty clear idea of what it is that remains to be done. Members made it clear that it was not my task as Chair to prescribe what is to be done next in a programmatic way. My task was to register where we are now, but I confess to having done so with an eye to genuinely clarifying where key convergences exist or key divergences remain, rather than obscuring or overcomplicating matters.

6. My own sense, when I review this myself, is the compelling urgency of seizing the moment and driving the process to a conclusion as rapidly as possible. We have made - particularly since August of this year - genuine and material progress. Indeed, it has come at a relatively rapid pace. It is also clear to me that it has been the product of a genuinely negotiating process. In other words, it has been a case of making proposals and counterproposals. That is why the matters covered in this report have an essentially conditional character. As I see it, the reality is that we have yet to find that last bridge to agreement that we need to secure modalities. But it would be a grave error, in my view, to imagine that we can take much time to find that bridge. As Chair, I am convinced that we must maintain momentum. You don't close divergences by taking time off to have a cup of tea. If you do so, you will find that everyone has moved backwards in the meantime. That, it seems to me, is a profound risk to our process. I would like to believe that this report at least underlines to us that there is indeed something real and important still within our grasp and we ought not to risk losing it. Our over-riding challenge and responsibility is to meet the development objective of the Doha Development Agenda. To meet this challenge and achieve this goal, we must act decisively and with real urgency.

7. The future life of this paper, if any, is a matter entirely in the hands of TNC Members to decide. This, as I see it, is the proper safeguard of the integrity of what has come to be described as a "bottom-up" process.

DOMESTIC SUPPORT

8. There has been very considerable potential convergence, albeit on a manifestly conditional basis.

Overall Cut

- There is a working hypothesis of three bands for overall cuts by developed countries. There is a strongly convergent working hypothesis that the thresholds for the three bands be US$ billion 0-10; 10-60; >60. On this basis, the European Communities would be in the top band, the United States and Japan in the second band, and all other developed countries at least in the third band. For developing countries, there is a view that either developing countries are assigned to the relevant integrated band (the bottom) or that there is a separate band for them.[1]

- Based on post-July 2005 proposals, there has been an undeniably significant convergence on the range of cuts. Of course, this has been conditional. But subject to that feature, a great deal of progress has been made since the bare bones of the July 2004 Framework. The following matrix provides a snapshot:

Bands	Thresholds (US$ billion)	Cuts
1	0-10	31%-70%
2	10-60	53%-75%
3	> 60	70%-80%

De Minimis

- On product-specific *de minimis* and non-product-specific *de minimis*, there is a zone of engagement for cuts between 50% and 80% for developed countries.

- As regards developing countries, there are still divergences to be bridged. In addition to the exemption specifically provided for in the Framework, there is a view that, for all developing countries, there should be no cut in *de minimis* at all. Alternatively, at least for those with no AMS, there should be no cut and, in any case, any cut for those with an AMS should be less than 2/3 of the cut for developed countries.

Blue Box

9.   There is important and significant convergence on moving beyond (i.e. further constraining) Blue Box programme payments envisaged in the July 2004 Framework.

However, the technique for achieving this remains to be determined. One proposal is to shrink the current 5% ceiling to 2.5%.[2] Another proposal rejects this in favour of additional criteria disciplining the so-called "new" Blue Box only. Others favour a combination of both, including additional disciplines on the "old" Blue Box.

AMS

- There is a working hypothesis of three bands for developed countries.

- There is close (but not full) convergence on the thresholds for those bands. There appears to be convergence that the top tier should be US$25 billion and above. There is some remaining divergence over the ceiling for the bottom band: between US$12 billion and 15 billion.

- There has been an undeniably significant convergence on the range of cuts. Of course, this has been conditional. But, that understood, a great deal of progress has been made since the bare bones of the July 2004 Framework. The following matrix[3] provides a snapshot:

Bands	Thresholds (US$ billion)	Cuts
1	0-12/15	37-60%
2	12/15-25	60-70%
3	>25	70-83%

- There is therefore working hypothesis agreement that the European Communities should be in the top tier, and the United States in the second tier. However, while the basis for Japan's placement as between these two tiers has been narrowed, it remains to be finally resolved.

- For developed countries in the bottom band, with a relatively high level of AMS relative to total value of agriculture production, there is emerging consensus that their band-related reduction should be complemented with an additional effort.

- What is needed now is a further step to bridge the remaining gap in positions - particularly as regards the United States and the European Communities, it being understood that this is not a matter to be resolved in isolation from the other elements in this pillar and beyond.

- On the base period for product-specific caps, certain proposals (such as for 1995-2000 and 1999-2001) are on the table. This needs to be resolved appropriately, including the manner in which special and differential treatment should be applied.

Green Box

10. The review and clarification commitment has not resulted in any discernible convergence on operational outcomes. There is, on the one side, a firm rejection of anything that is seen as departing from the existing disciplines while there is, on the other, an enduring sense that more could be done to review the Green Box without undermining ongoing reform. Beyond that there is, however, some tangible openness to finding appropriate ways to ensure that the Green Box is more "development friendly" i.e. better tailored to meet the realities of developing country agriculture but in a way that respects the fundamental requirement of at most minimal trade distortion.

EXPORT COMPETITION

End Date

11. While concrete proposals[4] have been made on the issue of an end date for elimination of all forms of export subsidies, there is at this stage no convergence. There are suggestions for the principle of front-loading or accelerated elimination for specific products, including particularly cotton.

Export Credits

12. Convergence has been achieved on a number of elements of disciplines with respect to export credits, export credit guarantee or insurance programmes with repayment periods of 180 days and below. However, a number of critical issues remain.[5]

Exporting State Trading Enterprises

13. There has been material convergence on rules to address trade-distorting practices identified in the July 2004 Framework text, although there are still major differences regarding the scope of practices to be covered by the new disciplines. Fundamentally opposing positions remain, however, on the issue of the future use of monopoly powers. There have been concrete drafting proposals on such matters as definition of entities and practices to be addressed as well as transparency. But there has been no genuine convergence in such areas.

Food Aid

14.   There is consensus among Members that the WTO shall not stand in the way of the provision of genuine food aid. There is also consensus that what is to be eliminated is commercial displacement. There have been detailed and intensive discussions, some of which have even been text-based, but not to a point where a consolidated draft text could be developed. This has been precluded by Members clinging to fundamentally disparate conceptual premises. There are proposals that in the disciplines a distinction should be made between at least two types of food aid: emergency food aid and food aid to address other situations. However, there is not yet a common understanding where emergency food aid ends and other food aid begins, reflecting concerns that this distinction should not become a means to create a loophole in disciplines. A fundamental sticking point is whether, except in exceptional, genuine emergency situations, Members should (albeit gradually) move towards untied, in-cash food aid only, as some Members propose but other Members strongly oppose.[6]

Special and Differential Treatment

15.   Framework provisions for special and differential treatment, including with respect to the monopoly status of state trading enterprises in developing countries and an extended lifetime for Article 9.4, have been uncontroversial, but details remain to be established.

Special Circumstances

16.   Work on the criteria and consultation procedures to govern any ad hoc temporary financing arrangements relating to exports to developing countries in exceptional circumstances is not much developed.

MARKET ACCESS

Tiered Formula

-       We have progressed on *ad valorem* equivalents.[7] This has successfully created a basis for allocating items into bands for the tiered formula.

-       We have a working hypothesis of four bands for structuring tariff cuts.

-       There has been very considerable convergence on adopting a linear-based approach for cuts within those bands. Members have, of course, by no means formally abandoned positions that are even more divergent.[8] We need now to narrow the extent of divergence that remains. This will include whether or not to include any "pivot" in any band.

–   Members have made strong efforts to promote convergence on the size of actual cuts to be undertaken within those bands. But, even though genuine efforts have been made to move from formal positions (which of course remain), major gaps are yet to be bridged. Somewhat greater convergence has been achieved as regards the thresholds for the bands. Substantial movement is clearly essential to progress.[9]

–   Some Members continue to reject completely the concept of a tariff cap. Others have proposed[10] a cap between 75-100%.

Sensitive Products

–   Members have been prepared to make concrete - albeit conditional - proposals on the number of sensitive products. But, in a situation where proposals extend from as little as 1% to as much as 15% of tariff lines, further bridging this difference is essential to progress.

–   The fundamental divergence over the basic approach to treatment of sensitive products needs to be resolved.[11] Beyond that, there needs to be convergence on the consequential extent of liberalisation for such products.

Special and Differential Treatment

–   Just as for developed countries, there is a working hypothesis of four bands for developing countries. There is no disagreement on lesser cuts within the bands. A certain body of opinion is open to considering cuts of two-thirds of the amount of the cuts for developed countries as a plausible zone in which to search more intensively for convergence.[12] But significant disagreement on that remains, and divergence is, if anything, somewhat more marked on the connected issue of higher thresholds for developing countries.[13]

–   Some Members continue to reject completely the concept of a tariff cap for developing countries. Others have proposed[14] a cap at 150%.

–   For sensitive products, there is no disagreement that there should be greater flexibility for developing countries, but the extent of this needs to be further defined.[15]

Special Products

–   Regarding *designation* of special products, there has been a clear divergence between those Members which consider that, prior to establishment of schedules, a list of non-exhaustive and illustrative criteria-based indicators should be established and those Members which are looking for a list which would act as a filter or screen for the selection of such products. Latterly, it has been proposed (but not yet discussed with Members as a whole) that a developing country Member should have the right to designate at least 20 per cent of its agricultural tariff lines as Special Products, and be further entitled to designate an SP where, for that product, an AMS has been notified and exports have taken place. This issue needs to be resolved as part of modalities so that there is assurance of the basis upon which Members may designate special products.

–   Some moves toward convergence on *treatment* of Special Products have been made recently. Some Members had considered that special products should be fully exempt from any new market access commitments whatsoever and have automatic access to the SSM. Others had argued there should be some degree of market opening for these products, albeit reflecting more flexible treatment than for other products. In the presence of this fundamental divergence, it had clearly been impossible to undertake any definition of what such flexibility would be. Genuine convergence is obviously urgently needed. There is now a new proposal for a tripartite categorization of Special Products involving limited tariff cuts for at least a proportion of such products which remains to be fully discussed. It remains to be seen whether this discussion can help move us forward.

Special Safeguard Mechanism

–   There is agreement that there would be a special safeguard mechanism and that it should be tailored to the particular circumstances and needs of developing countries. There is no material disagreement with the view that it should have a quantity trigger. Nor is there disagreement with the view that it should at least be capable of addressing effectively what might be described as import "surges". Divergence remains over whether, or if so how, situations that are lesser than "surge" are to be dealt with. There is, however, agreement that any remedy should be of a temporary nature. There remains strong divergence however on whether, or if so how, a special safeguard should be "price-based" to deal specifically with price effects.

–   There is some discernible openness, albeit at varying levels, to at least consider coverage of products that are likely to undergo significant liberalisation effects, and/or are already bound at low levels and/or are special products. Beyond that, however, there remains a fundamental divergence between those considering all products should be eligible for such a mechanism and those opposing such a blanket approach.

Other Elements

17.   There has been no further material convergence on the matters covered by paragraphs 35 and 37 of the July 2004 Framework text. The same may be said for paragraph 36 on tariff escalation, albeit that there is full agreement on the need for this to be done, and a genuine recognition of the particular importance of this for commodities exporters. Certain concrete proposals have been made on paragraph 38 (SSG) and met with opposition from some Members.

18.   Concrete proposals have been made and discussed on how to implement paragraph 43 of the July 2004 Framework on tropical and diversification products. But there remains divergence over the precise interpretation of this section of the July Framework[16] and no common approach has been established.

19.   The importance of long-standing preferences pursuant to paragraph 44 of the July 2004 Framework is fully recognised and concrete proposals regarding preference erosion have been made and discussed.[17] There seems not to be inherent difficulty with a role for capacity building. However, while there is some degree of support for e.g. longer implementation periods for at least certain products in order to facilitate adjustment, there is far from convergence on even this. Some argue it is not sufficient or certainly not in all cases, while others that it is not warranted at all.

LEAST-DEVELOPED COUNTRIES

20.   There is no questioning of the terms of paragraph 45 of the July Framework agreement, which exempts least-developed countries from any reduction requirement. The stipulation that "developed Members, and developing country Members in a position to do so, should provide duty-free and quota-free market access for products originating from least-developed countries" is not at this point concretely operational for all Members. At this stage, several Members have made undertakings. Proposals for this to be bound remain on the table.[18]

COTTON

21.   While there is genuine recognition of the problem to be addressed and concrete proposals have been made, Members remain at this point short of concrete and specific achievement that would be needed to meet the July Framework direction to address this matter ambitiously, expeditiously and specifically. There is no disagreement with the view that all forms of export subsidies are to be eliminated for cotton although the timing and speed remains to be specified. Proposals to eliminate them immediately or from day one of the implementation period are not at this point shared by all Members. In the case of trade distorting support, proponents seek full elimination with "front-loaded" implementation.[19] There is a view that the extent to which this can occur, and its timing, can only be determined in the context of an overall agreement. Another view is that there could be at least substantial and front-loaded reduction on cotton specifically from day one of implementation, with the major implementation achieved within twelve months, and the remainder to be completed within a period shorter than the overall implementation period for agriculture.[20]

RECENTLY-ACCEDED MEMBERS

22.   Concrete proposals have been made and discussed, but no specific flexibility provisions have commanded consensus.

MONITORING AND SURVEILLANCE

23.   A proposal has been made but there is no material advance at this point.

OTHER ISSUES

24.   On paragraph 49 (sectoral initiatives, differential export taxes, GIs) certain positions and proposals have been tabled and/or referred to. They are issues that remain of interest but not agreed.

25.   At this point, proposals on paragraph 50 have not advanced materially.

26.   In the case of small and vulnerable economies, a concrete proposal has been made recently. It has not yet been subject to consultation.

27.   There is openness to the particular concerns of commodity-dependent developing and least-developed countries facing long-term decline and/or sharp fluctuations in prices. There is, at this point (where, overall, precise modalities are still pending), support for the view that such modalities should eventually be capable of addressing effectively key areas for them.[21]

Notes

1 On the proposed basis that cut remains to be determined for those developing countries with an AMS. In any case, there is a view (not shared by all) that cuts for developing countries should be less than 2/3 of the cut for developed countries.

2 The exact extent of the flexibility to be provided pursuant to paragraph 15 of the July 2004 Framework remains to be agreed.

3 Of course, this needs to be viewed as illustrative rather than overly literally, if for no other reason than that these are conditional figures. For instance, while the European Communities has indicated it could be prepared to go as far as 70% in the top tier, they make it clear that this is acceptable only if the United States will go to 60% in the second tier. The United States for its part, however, has only indicated preparedness to go to that 60% if the European Communities is prepared to go as high as 83% - which it has not indicated it is prepared to do.

4 One Member has proposed the year 2010 for "export subsidies", with accelerated elimination for "specific" products. Another group of Members have proposed a period "no longer than five years" for all forms of export subsidies, with "direct" export subsidies subject to front-loading within that period.

5 This includes, but is not limited to: exemptions, if any, to the 180 day rule; whether the disciplines should allow for pure cover only or also permit direct financing; the appropriate period for programmes to fully recover their costs and losses through the premia levied from the exporters (principle of self-financing - there needs to be convergence between position which range from one year to fifteen years); the disciplines regarding special circumstances; and the question of special and differential treatment, including whether, as some Members argue, developing countries should be allowed longer repayment terms for export credits extended by them to other developing countries and the specifics of differential treatment in favour of least-developed and net food-importing developing countries.

6 This fundamental divergence has effectively precluded convergence on such matters as what disciplines, if any, should be established with respect to monetization of food aid or the question of the provision of food aid in fully grant form only. The importance of operationally effective transparency requirements is generally acknowledged, but details have still to be developed, particularly those relating to the role of the WTO in this context. Further work is required to clarify the role of recipient countries and relevant international organizations or other entities in triggering or providing food aid.

7 The method for calculating the AVEs for the sugar lines is still to be established.

8 At one end of the spectrum, as it were, a "harmonisation" formula within the bands; at the other end "flexibility" within the formula.

9 The matrix below is an illustrative table that portrays the extent of divergences that remain, even on the basis of post-August 2005 proposals. This does not entirely cover all the subtleties of those proposals to utilize a "pivot" (although most are in fact within the ranges tabulated), but is intended to convey a snapshot of the status of average cuts proposed post-August.

	Thresholds	Range of cuts (%)
Band 1	0%–20/30%	20–65
Band 2	20/30%–40/60%	30–75
Band 3	40/60%–60/90%	35–85
Band 4	>60/90%	42–90

10 As an element in certain conditional proposals on overall market access, tabled post-July 2005.

11 Some see this as being tariff quota based and expressed as a percentage of domestic consumption, with proposals of up to 10%. Others propose *pro rata* expansion on an existing trade basis, including taking account of current imports. Some also propose no new TRQs, with sensitivity in such cases to be provided through other means, e.g. differential phasing. There is also a proposal for a "sliding scale" approach.

12 In this pillar, as well as in the other two, there is general convergence on the point that developing countries will have entitlement to longer implementation periods, albeit that concrete precision remains to be determined.

13 The matrix below is an illustrative table that portrays the extent of divergences that remain, just on the basis of post-August 2005 proposals.

	Thresholds	Range of cuts (%)
Band 1	0%–20/50%	15-25*
Band 2	20/50%–40/100%	20-30*
Band 3	40/100%–60/150%	25-35*
Band 4	>60-150%	30-40*

* There is also a proposal that cuts for developing countries should be "slightly lesser" than the upper tariff cuts for developed countries shown in the preceding table (i.e.: "slightly lesser" than 65, 75, 85 and 90%).

[14] As an element in certain conditional proposals on overall market access, tabled post-July 2005.

[15] While the eventual zone of convergence for developed countries undoubtedly has a bearing in this area, it has been proposed by a group of Members that the principles of sensitive products generally and for TRQs specifically should be different for developing countries. Another group of Members has proposed, in the post-August period, an entitlement for developing countries of at least 50% more than the maximum number of lines used by any developed Member. This would (based on developed country proposals) amount to a potential variation between 1.5% and 22.5% of tariff lines. This latter group has also proposed that products relating to long-standing preferences shall be designated as sensitive and that any TRQ expansion should not be "at the detriment of existing ACP quotas". This particular view has been, however, strongly opposed by other Members which take the firm position that tropical and diversification products should not at all be designated as sensitive products.

[16] It is argued by some Members that this is to be interpreted as meaning full duty- and tariff quota-free access, but by others as less than that.

[17] Note 15 above refers.

[18] It is also proposed that this should be accompanied by simple and transparent rules of origin and other measures to address non-tariff barriers.

[19] Concrete proposals have been made, with a three-step approach: 80% on day one, an additional 10% after 12 months and the last 10% a year later.

[20] A Member has indicated that it is prepared to implement all its commitments from day one and, in any case, to autonomously ensure that its commitments on eliminating the most trade-distorting domestic support, eliminating all forms of export subsidies and providing mfn duty- and quota-free access for cotton will take place from 2006.

[21] This would appear to include in particular such a matter as tariff escalation, where it discourages the development of processing industries in the commodity producing countries. The idea of a review and clarification of what the current status is of GATT 1994 provisions relating to the stabilisation of prices through the adoption of supply management systems by producing countries, and the use of export taxes and restrictions under such systems is also on the table. Proponents would seek something more than this such as more concrete undertakings in the area of non-tariff measures and actual revision of existing provisions. There is, at this point, no consensus in these latter areas, but an appreciation at least of the underlying issues at stake.

Annex B

Market Access for Non-Agricultural Products
Report by the Chairman of the Negotiating Group on Market Access to the TNC

A.   INTRODUCTION

1.   A Chairman's commentary of the state of play of the NAMA negotiations was prepared in July 2005 and circulated in document JOB(05)/147 and Add.1 (hereinafter referred to as the "Chairman's commentary"). The current report, made on my responsibility, reflects the state of play of the NAMA negotiations at this juncture of the Doha Development Agenda, and supplements that commentary.

2.   With an eye on the forthcoming Ministerial, Section B of this report attempts to highlight those areas of convergence and divergence on the elements of Annex B of Decision adopted by the General Council on 1 August 2004, (hereinafter referred to as the "NAMA framework"), and to provide some guidance as to what may be a possible future course of action with respect to some of the elements. Section C of the report provides some final remarks about possible action by Ministers at Hong Kong.

3.   In preparing this report, use has been made of documents provided by Members (as listed in TN/MA/S/16/Rev.2) as well as the discussions in the open-ended sessions of the Group, plurilateral meetings and bilateral contacts, as long as they were not in the nature of confessionals.

B.   SUMMARY OF THE STATE OF PLAY

4.   Full modalities must have detailed language and, where required, final numbers on all elements of the NAMA framework. Such an agreement should also contain a detailed work plan concerning the process after the establishment of full modalities for the purpose of the submission, verification and annexation of Doha Schedules to a legal instrument. While acknowledging that progress has been made since the adoption of the NAMA framework, the establishment of full modalities is, at present, a difficult prospect given the lack of agreement on a number of elements in the NAMA framework including the formula, paragraph 8 flexibilities and unbound tariffs.

5.   Regarding the structure of this section, generally Members recognize that the issues identified in the preceding paragraph are the three elements of the NAMA framework on

which solutions are required as a matter of priority, and that there is a need to address them in an interlinked fashion. So, this report will commence with these three subjects before moving on to the other elements of the NAMA framework in the order in which they are presented therein.

Formula (paragraph 4 of the NAMA framework)

6.   On the non-linear formula, there has been movement since the adoption of the NAMA framework. There is a more common understanding of the shape of the formula that Members are willing to adopt in these negotiations. In fact, Members have been focusing on a Swiss formula. During the past few months, much time and effort has been spent examining the impact of such a formula from both a defensive and offensive angle. In terms of the specifics of that formula, there are basically two variations on the table: a formula with a limited number of negotiated coefficients and a formula where the value of each country's coefficient would be based essentially on the tariff average of bound rates of that Member, resulting in multiple coefficients.

7.   In order to move beyond a debate on the merits of the two options (and in recognition of the fact that what matters in the final analysis is the level of the coefficient) more recently Members have engaged in a discussion of numbers. Such a debate has been particularly helpful, especially as it demonstrated in a quantifiable manner to what extent the benchmarks established in paragraph 16 of the Doha Ministerial Declaration would be achieved. While it is evident that one of the characteristics of such a formula is to address tariff peaks, tariff escalation and high tariffs (as it brings down high tariffs more than low tariffs), one benchmark which has been the subject of differences of opinion has been that of "less than full reciprocity in reduction commitments" and how it should be measured. Some developing Members are of the view that this means less than average percentage cuts i.e. as translated through a higher coefficient in the formula, than those undertaken by developed country Members. However, the latter have indicated that there are other measurements of less than full reciprocity in reduction commitments including the final rates after the formula cut which in their markets would be less than in developing country markets. Also, in their view, such a measurement of less than full reciprocity in reduction commitments has to take into account not only the additional effort made by them in all areas but also of paragraph 8 flexibilities and the fact that several developing Members and the LDCs would be exempt from formula cuts.

8.   Other objectives put forward by developed Members and some developing Members as being part of the Doha NAMA mandate are: harmonization of tariffs between Members;

cuts into applied rates; and improvement of South-South trade. However, these objectives have been challenged by other developing Members who believe that, on the contrary, they are not part of that mandate.

9.   During the informal discussions, many Members engaged in an exchange on the basis of an approach with two coefficients. In the context of such debates, the coefficients which were mentioned for developed Members fell generally within the range of 5 to 10, and for developing Members within the range of 15 to 30, although some developing Members did propose lower coefficients for developed Members and higher coefficients for developing Members. In addition, a developing country coefficient of 10 was also put forward by some developed Members. However, while this discussion of numbers is a positive development, the inescapable reality is that the range of coefficients is wide and reflects the divergence that exists as to Members' expectations regarding the contributions that their trading partners should be making.

Flexibilities for developing Members subject to a formula (paragraph 8 of the NAMA framework)

10.   A central issue concerning the paragraph 8 flexibilities has been the question of linkage or non-linkage between these flexibilities and the coefficient in the formula. A view was expressed that the flexibilities currently provided for in paragraph 8 are equivalent to 4-5 additional points to the coefficient in the formula, and as a result there was need to take this aspect into account in the developing country coefficient. In response, the argument has been made by many developing Members that those flexibilities are a stand alone provision as reflected in the language of that provision, and should not be linked to the coefficient. Otherwise, this would amount to re-opening the NAMA framework. Some of those Members have also expressed the view that the numbers currently within square brackets are the minimum required for their sensitive tariff lines, and have expressed concern about the conditions attached to the use of such flexibilities, such as the capping of the import value. In response, the point has been made by developed Members that they are not seeking to remove the flexibilities under paragraph 8, and therefore are not re-opening the NAMA framework. They further point out that the numbers in paragraph 8 are within square brackets precisely to reflect the fact that they are not fixed and may need to be adjusted downwards depending on the level of the coefficient. In addition, the need for more transparency and predictability with regard to the tariff lines which would be covered by paragraph 8 flexibilities has been raised by some of these Members. Some developing Members have also advanced the idea that there should be the option for

those developing Members not wanting to use paragraph 8 flexibilities to have recourse to a higher coefficient in the formula in the interest of having a balanced outcome.

Unbound Tariff Lines (paragraph 5, indent two of the NAMA framework)

11.   There has been progress on the discussion of unbound tariff lines. There is an understanding that full bindings would be a desirable objective of the NAMA negotiations, and a growing sense that unbound tariff lines should be subject to formula cuts provided there is a pragmatic solution for those lines with low applied rates. However, some Members have stressed that their unbound tariff lines with high applied rates are also sensitive and due consideration should be given to those lines. There now appears to be a willingness among several Members to move forward on the basis of a non-linear mark-up approach to establish base rates, and in the case of some of these Members, provided that such an approach yields an equitable result. A non-linear mark-up approach envisages the addition of a certain number of percentage points to the applied rate of the unbound tariff line in order to establish the base rate on which the formula is to be applied. There are two variations of such an approach. In one case, a constant number of percentage points are added to the applied rate in order to establish the base rate. The other variation consists of having a different number of percentage points depending on the level of the applied rate. In other words, the lower the applied rate the higher the mark-up and the higher the applied rate, the lower the mark-up. There is also one proposal on the table of a target average approach where an average is established through the use of a formula, with the unbound tariff lines expected to have final bindings around that average.

12.   On a practical level, in their discussions on unbound tariff lines, Members have been referring mostly to the constant mark-up methodology to establish base rates. In the context of such discussions, the number for the mark-up has ranged from 5 to 30 percentage points. Once again the gap between the two figures is wide, but Members have displayed willingness to be flexible.

Other elements of the formula (paragraph 5 of the NAMA framework)

13.   Concerning product coverage (indent 1), Members have made good progress to establish a list of non-agricultural products as reflected in document JOB(05)/226/Rev.2. The main issue is whether the outcome of this exercise should be an agreed list or guidelines. It would appear that several Members are in favour of the former outcome, however, some have expressed their preference for the latter. In any event, there are only a limited number of items (17) on which differences exist and Members should try and resolve these differences as quickly as possible.

14.   On *ad valorem* equivalents (indent 5), agreement was reached to convert non *ad valorem* duties to *ad valorem* equivalents on the basis of the methodology contained in JOB(05)/166/Rev.1 and to bind them in *ad valorem* terms. To date, four Members have submitted their preliminary AVE calculations, but there are many more due. Those Members would need to submit this information as quickly as possible so as to allow sufficient time for the multilateral verification process.

15.   The subject of how credit is to be given for autonomous liberalization (indent 4) by developing countries provided that the tariff lines are bound on an MFN basis in the WTO since the conclusion of the Uruguay Round has not been discussed in detail since the adoption of the NAMA framework. However, this issue may be more usefully taken up once there is a clearer picture of the formula.

16.   All the other elements of the formula such as tariff cuts commencing from bound rates after full implementation of current commitments (indent 2), the base year (indent 3), the nomenclature (indent 6) and reference period for import data (indent 7) have not been discussed any further since July 2004, as they were acceptable to Members as currently reflected in the NAMA framework.

Other flexibilities for developing Members

Members with low binding coverage (paragraph 6 of the NAMA framework)

17.   A submission by a group of developing Members, covered under paragraph 6 provisions, was made in June 2005. The paper proposed that Members falling under this paragraph should be encouraged to substantially increase their binding coverage, and bind tariff lines at a level consistent with their individual development, trade, fiscal and strategic needs. A preliminary discussion of this proposal revealed that there were concerns about this proposal re-opening this paragraph by seeking to enhance the flexibilities contained therein. Further discussion of this proposal is required. However, it appears that the issue of concern to some of the paragraph 6 Members is not related so much to the full binding coverage, but rather to the average level at which these Members would be required to bind their tariffs.

Flexibilities for LDCs (paragraph 9 of the NAMA framework)

18.   There appears to be a common understanding that LDCs will be the judge of the extent and level of the bindings that they make. At the same time, Members have indicated that this substantial increase of the binding commitments which LDCs are expected to undertake should be done with a good faith effort. In this regard, some

yardsticks for this effort were mentioned including the coverage and level of bindings made in the Uruguay Round by other LDCs as well as the more recently acceded LDCs.

Small, vulnerable economies

19. A paper was submitted recently by a group of Members which proposes *inter alia* lesser and linear cuts to Members identified by a criterion using trade share. While some developing and developed Members were sympathetic to the situation of such Members, concerns were expressed with respect to the threshold used to establish eligibility, and also the treatment envisaged. Other developing Members expressed serious reservations about this proposal which in their view appeared to be creating a new category of developing Members, and to be further diluting the ambition of the NAMA negotiations. The sponsors of this proposal stressed that the small, vulnerable economies had characteristics which warranted special treatment.

20. This is an issue on which there is a serious divergence of opinion among developing Members. This subject will need to be debated further. Discussions may be facilitated through additional statistical analysis.

Sectorals (paragraph 7 of the NAMA framework)

21. It appears that good progress is being made on the sectoral tariff component of the NAMA negotiations. Work which is taking place in an informal Member-driven process has focused on *inter alia* identification of sectors, product coverage, participation, end rates and adequate provisions of flexibilities for developing countries. Besides the sectorals based on a critical mass approach identified in the Chairman's commentary - bicycles, chemicals, electronics/electrical equipment, fish, footwear, forest products, gems and jewellery, pharmaceuticals and medical equipment, raw materials and sporting goods - I understand that work is ongoing on other sectors namely apparel, auto/auto parts and textiles.

22. While this component of the NAMA negotiations is recognized in the NAMA framework to be a key element to delivering on the objectives of paragraph 16 of the Doha NAMA mandate, some developing Members have questioned the rationale of engaging in sectoral negotiations before having the formula finalized. Many have also re-iterated their view that sectorals are voluntary in nature. The point has also been made by other developing Members that sectorals harm smaller developing Members due to an erosion of their preferences. However, the proponents of such initiatives have argued that sectorals are another key element of the NAMA negotiations and an important modality for delivering on the elimination of duties as mandated in paragraph 16 of the Doha Ministerial Declaration.

In addition, they have pointed out that some of the sectorals were initiated by developing Members. Moreover, such initiatives require substantive work and were time-consuming to prepare. Concerning preference erosion, this was a cross-cutting issue.

23.   Members will need to begin considering time-lines for the finalization of such work, and the submission of the outcomes which will be applied on an MFN basis.

Market Access for LDCs (paragraph 10 of the NAMA framework)

24.   In the discussions on this subject, it was noted that the Committee on Trade and Development in Special Session is examining the question of duty-free and quota-free access for non-agricultural products originating from LDCs. Consequently, there is recognition by Members that the discussions in that Committee would most probably have an impact on this element of the NAMA framework, and would need to be factored in at the appropriate time.

Newly Acceded Members (paragraph 11 of the NAMA framework)

25.   Members recognize the extensive market access commitments made by the NAMs at the time of their accession. From the discussions held on this subject, it was clarified that those NAMs which are developing Members have access to paragraph 8 flexibilities. As special provisions for tariff reductions for the NAMs, some Members are willing to consider longer implementation periods than those to be provided to developing Members. Other proposals such as a higher coefficient and "grace periods" for the NAMs were also put forward, but a number of Members have objected to these ideas. There has also been a submission by four low-income economies in transition who have requested to be exempt from formula cuts in light of their substantive contributions at the time of their WTO accession and the current difficult state of their economies. While some Members showed sympathy for the situation of these Members, they expressed the view that other solutions may be more appropriate. Some developing Members also expressed concern about this proposal creating a differentiation between Members. Further discussion is required on these issues.

NTBs (paragraph 14 of the NAMA framework)

26.   Since adoption of the July 2004 framework, Members have been focusing their attention on non-tariff barriers in recognition of the fact that they are an integral and equally important part of the NAMA negotiations. Some Members claim that they constitute a greater barrier to their exports than tariffs. The Group has spent a considerable amount of time identifying, categorizing and examining the notified NTBs. Members are using bilateral, vertical and horizontal approaches to the NTB negotiations. For example, many Members

are raising issues bilaterally with their trading partners. Vertical initiatives are ongoing on automobiles, electronic products and wood products. There have been some proposals of a horizontal nature concerning export taxes, export restrictions and remanufactured products. On export taxes, some Members have expressed the view that such measures fall outside the mandate of the NAMA negotiations. Some Members have also raised in other Negotiating Groups some of the NTBs they had notified initially in the context of the NAMA negotiations. For example, a number of trade facilitation measures are now being examined in the Negotiating Group on Trade Facilitation. Some other Members have also indicated their intention to bring issues to the regular WTO Committees. NTBs currently proposed for negotiation in the NAMA Group are contained in document JOB(05)/85/Rev.3.

27.   Some proposals have been made of a procedural nature in order to expedite the NTB work, including a suggestion to hold dedicated NTB sessions. Further consideration will need to be given to this and other proposals. Members will also need to begin considering some time-lines for the submission of specific negotiating proposals and NTB outcomes.

Appropriate Studies and Capacity Building Measures (paragraph 15 of the NAMA framework)

28.   There has been no discussion as such on this element as it is an ongoing and integral part of the negotiating process. Several papers have been prepared by the Secretariat during the course of the negotiations and capacity building activities by the Secretariat have increased considerably since the launch of the Doha Development Agenda. Such activities will need to continue taking into account the evolution of the negotiations.

Non-reciprocal preferences (paragraph 16 of the NAMA framework)

29.   In response to calls by some Members for a better idea of the scope of the problem, the ACP Group circulated an indicative list of products (170 HS 6-digit tariff lines) vulnerable to preference erosion in the EC and US markets as identified through a vulnerability index. Simulations were also submitted by the African Group. Some developing Members expressed concern that the tariff lines listed covered the majority of their exports, or covered critical exports to those markets and were also precisely the lines on which they sought MFN cuts. As a result, for these Members, it was impossible to entertain any solution which related to less than full formula cuts or longer staging. In this regard, concern was expressed by them that non-trade solutions were not being examined. For the proponents of the issue, a trade solution was necessary as this was a trade problem. According to them, their proposal would

not undermine trade liberalization because they were seeking to manage such liberalization on a limited number of products.

30.   This subject is highly divisive precisely because the interests of the two groups of developing Members are in direct conflict. Additionally, it is a cross-cutting issue which makes it even more sensitive. While, the aforementioned list of products has been helpful in providing a sense of the scope of the problem and may help Members to engage in a more focused discussion, it is clear that pragmatism will need to be shown by all concerned.

Environmental Goods (paragraph 17 of the NAMA framework)

31.   Since the adoption of the July framework in 2004, limited discussions have been held on this subject in the Group. However, it is noted that much work under paragraph 31(iii) of the Doha Ministerial Declaration has been undertaken by the Committee on Trade and Environment in Special Session. There would need to be close coordination between the two negotiating groups and a stock taking of the work undertaken in that Committee would be required at the appropriate time by the NAMA Negotiating Group.

Other elements of the NAMA framework

32.   On the other elements of the NAMA framework, such as supplementary modalities (paragraph 12), elimination of low duties (paragraph 13) and tariff revenue dependency (paragraph 16) the Group has not had a substantive debate. This has in part to do with the nature of the issue or because more information is required from the proponents. Regarding supplementary modalities, such modalities will become more relevant once the formula has been finalized. On elimination of low duties, this issue may be more suitable to consider once there is a better sense of the likely outcome of the NAMA negotiations. On tariff revenue dependency, more clarity is required from the proponents on the nature and scope of the problem.

C.   FINAL REMARKS

33.   As may be observed from the above report, Members are far away from achieving full modalities. This is highly troubling. It will take a major effort by all if the objective of concluding the NAMA negotiations by the end of 2006 is to be realized.

34.   To this end, I would highlight as a critical objective for Hong Kong a common understanding on the formula, paragraph 8 flexibilities and unbound tariffs. It is crucial that Ministers move decisively on these elements so that the overall outcome is acceptable to all.

This will give the necessary impetus to try and fulfil at a date soon thereafter the objective of full modalities for the NAMA negotiations.

35.   Specifically, Ministers should:

- Obtain agreement on the final structure of the formula and narrow the range of numbers.

- Resolve their basic differences over paragraph 8 flexibilities.

- Clarify whether the constant mark-up approach is the way forward, and if so, narrow the range of numbers.

Annex C

Services

Objectives

1.   In order to achieve a progressively higher level of liberalization of trade in services, with appropriate flexibility for individual developing country Members, we agree that Members should be guidd, to the maximum extent possible, by the following objectives in making their new and improved commitments:

(a)   Mode 1

(i)   commitments at existing levels of market access on a non-discriminatory basis across sectors of interest to Members

(ii)   removal of existing requirements of commercial presence

(b)   Mode 2

(i)   commitments at existing levels of market access on a non-discriminatory basis across sectors of interest to Members

(ii)   commitments on mode 2 where commitments on mode 1 exist

(c)   Mode 3

(i)   commitments on enhanced levels of foreign equity participation

(ii)   removal or substantial reduction of economic needs tests

(iii)   commitments allowing greater flexibility on the types of legal entity permitted

(d)   Mode 4

(i)   new or improved commitments on the categories of Contractual Services Suppliers, Independent Professionals and Others, de-linked from commercial presence, to reflect *inter alia*:

—   removal or substantial reduction of economic needs tests

—   indication of prescribed duration of stay and possibility of renewal, if any

    (ii)   new or improved commitments on the categories of Intra-corporate Transferees and Business Visitors, to reflect *inter alia*:

        –   removal or substantial reduction of economic needs tests

        –   indication of prescribed duration of stay and possibility of renewal, if any

  (e)   MFN Exemptions

    (i)   removal or substantial reduction of exemptions from most-favoured-nation (MFN) treatment

    (ii)   clarification of remaining MFN exemptions in terms of scope of application and duration

  (f)   Scheduling of Commitments

    (i)   ensuring clarity, certainty, comparability and coherence in the scheduling and classification of commitments through adherence to, *inter alia*, the Scheduling Guidelines pursuant to the Decision of the Council for Trade in Services adopted on 23 March 2001

    (ii)   ensuring that scheduling of any remaining economic needs tests adheres to the Scheduling Guidelines pursuant to the Decision of the Council for Trade in Services adopted on 23 March 2001.

2.   As a reference for the request-offer negotiations, the sectoral and modal objectives as identified by Members may be considered.[1]

3.   Members shall pursue full and effective implementation of the Modalities for the Special Treatment for Least-Developed Country Members in the Negotiations on Trade in Services (LDC Modalities) adopted by the Special Session of the Council for Trade in Services on 3 September 2003, with a view to the beneficial and meaningful integration of LDCs into the multilateral trading system.

4.   Members must intensify their efforts to conclude the negotiations on rule-making under GATS Articles X, XIII, and XV in accordance with their respective mandates and timelines:

(a)   Members should engage in more focused discussions in connection with the technical and procedural questions relating to the operation and application of any possible emergency safeguard measures in services.

(b)   On government procurement, Members should engage in more focused discussions and in this context put greater emphasis on proposals by Members, in accordance with Article XIII of the GATS.

(c)   On subsidies, Members should intensify their efforts to expedite and fulfil the information exchange required for the purpose of such negotiations, and should engage in more focused discussions on proposals by Members, including the development of a possible working definition of subsidies in services.

5.   Members shall develop disciplines on domestic regulation pursuant to the mandate under Article VI:4 of the GATS before the end of the current round of negotiations. We call upon Members to develop text for adoption. In so doing, Members shall consider proposals and the illustrative list of possible elements for Article VI:4 disciplines.[2]

Approaches

6.   Pursuant to the principles and objectives above, we agree to intensify and expedite the request-offer negotiations, which shall remain the main method of negotiation, with a view to securing substantial commitments.

7.   In addition to bilateral negotiations, we agree that the request-offer negotiations should also be pursued on a plurilateral basis in accordance with the principles of the GATS and the Guidelines and Procedures for the Negotiations on Trade in Services. The results of such negotiations shall be extended on an MFN basis. These negotiations would be organized in the following manner:

(a)   Any Member or group of Members may present requests or collective requests to other Members in any specific sector or mode of supply, identifying their objectives for the negotiations in that sector or mode of supply.

(b)   Members to whom such requests have been made shall consider such requests in accordance with paragraphs 2 and 4 of Article XIX of the GATS and paragraph 11 of the Guidelines and Procedures for the Negotiations on Trade in Services.

(c)   Plurilateral negotiations should be organised with a view to facilitating the participation of all Members, taking into account the limited capacity of developing countries and smaller delegations to participate in such negotiations.

8.   Due consideration shall be given to proposals on trade-related concerns of small economies.

9.   Members, in the course of negotiations, shall develop methods for the full and effective implementation of the LDC Modalities, including expeditiously:

(a)   Developing appropriate mechanisms for according special priority including to sectors and modes of supply of interest to LDCs in accordance with Article IV:3 of the GATS and paragraph 7 of the LDC Modalities.

(b)   Undertaking commitments, to the extent possible, in such sectors and modes of supply identified, or to be identified, by LDCs that represent priority in their development policies in accordance with paragraphs 6 and 9 of the LDC Modalities.

(c)   Assisting LDCs to enable them to identify sectors and modes of supply that represent development priorities.

(d)   Providing targeted and effective technical assistance and capacity building for LDCs in accordance with the LDC Modalities, particularly paragraphs 8 and 12.

(e)   Developing a reporting mechanism to facilitate the review requirement in paragraph 13 of the LDC Modalities.

10.   Targeted technical assistance should be provided through, *inter alia*, the WTO Secretariat, with a view to enabling developing and least-developed countries to participate effectively in the negotiations. In particular and in accordance with paragraph 51 on Technical Cooperation of this Declaration, targeted technical assistance should be given to all developing countries allowing them to fully engage in the negotiation. In addition, such assistance should be provided on, *inter alia*, compiling and analyzing statistical data on trade in services, assessing interests in and gains from services trade, building regulatory capacity, particularly on those services sectors where liberalization is being undertaken by developing countries.

Timelines

11.   Recognizing that an effective timeline is necessary in order to achieve a successful conclusion of the negotiations, we agree that the negotiations shall adhere to the following dates:

     (a)   Any outstanding initial offers shall be submitted as soon as possible.

     (b)   Groups of Members presenting plurilateral requests to other Members should submit such requests by 28 February 2006 or as soon as possible thereafter.

     (c)   A second round of revised offers shall be submitted by 31 July 2006.

     (d)   Final draft schedules of commitments shall be submitted by 31 October 2006.

     (e)   Members shall strive to complete the requirements in 9(a) before the date in 11(c).

Review of Progress

12.   The Special Session of the Council for Trade in Services shall review progress in the negotiations and monitor the implementation of the Objectives, Approaches and Timelines set out in this Annex.

Notes

[1]   As attached to the Report by the Chairman to the Trade Negotiations Committee on 28 November 2005, contained in document TN/S/23. This attachment has no legal standing.

[2]   As attached to the Report of the Chairman of the Working Party on Domestic Regulation to the Special Session of the Council for Trade in Services on 15 November 2005, contained in document JOB(05)/280.

Annex D

Rules
I. Anti-Dumping and Subsidies and Countervailing Measures including Fisheries Subsidies

We:

1. *acknowledge* that the achievement of substantial results on all aspects of the Rules mandate, in the form of amendments to the Anti-Dumping (AD) and Subsidies and Countervailing Measures (SCM) Agreements, is important to the development of the rules-based multilateral trading system and to the overall balance of results in the DDA;

2. *aim* to achieve in the negotiations on Rules further improvements, in particular, to the transparency, predictability and clarity of the relevant disciplines, to the benefit of all Members, including in particular developing and least-developed Members. In this respect, the development dimension of the negotiations must be addressed as an integral part of any outcome;

3. *call on* Participants, in considering possible clarifications and improvements in the area of anti-dumping, to take into account, *inter alia*, (a) the need to avoid the unwarranted use of anti-dumping measures, while preserving the basic concepts, principles and effectiveness of the instrument and its objectives where such measures are warranted; and (b) the desirability of limiting the costs and complexity of proceedings for interested parties and the investigating authorities alike, while strengthening the due process, transparency and predictability of such proceedings and measures;

4. *consider* that negotiations on anti-dumping should, as appropriate, clarify and improve the rules regarding, *inter alia*, (a) determinations of dumping, injury and causation, and the application of measures; (b) procedures governing the initiation, conduct and completion of antidumping investigations, including with a view to strengthening due process and enhancing transparency; and (c) the level, scope and duration of measures, including duty assessment, interim and new shipper reviews, sunset, and anti-circumvention proceedings;

5. *recognize* that negotiations on anti-dumping have intensified and deepened, that Participants are showing a high level of constructive engagement, and

that the process of rigorous discussion of the issues based on specific textual proposals for amendment to the AD Agreement has been productive and is a necessary step in achieving the substantial results to which Ministers are committed;

6.   *note* that, in the negotiations on anti-dumping, the Negotiating Group on Rules has been discussing in detail proposals on such issues as determinations of injury/causation, the lesser duty rule, public interest, transparency and due process, interim reviews, sunset, duty assessment, circumvention, the use of facts available, limited examination and all others rates, dispute settlement, the definition of dumped imports, affiliated parties, product under consideration, and the initiation and completion of investigations, and that this process of discussing proposals before the Group or yet to be submitted will continue after Hong Kong;

7.   *note*, in respect of subsidies and countervailing measures, that while proposals for amendments to the SCM Agreement have been submitted on a number of issues, including the definition of a subsidy, specificity, prohibited subsidies, serious prejudice, export credits and guarantees, and the allocation of benefit, there is a need to deepen the analysis on the basis of specific textual proposals in order to ensure a balanced outcome in all areas of the Group's mandate;

8.   *note* the desirability of applying to both anti-dumping and countervailing measures any clarifications and improvements which are relevant and appropriate to both instruments;

9.   *recall* our commitment at Doha to enhancing the mutual supportiveness of trade and environment, *note* that there is broad agreement that the Group should strengthen disciplines on subsidies in the fisheries sector, including through the prohibition of certain forms of fisheries subsidies that contribute to overcapacity and over-fishing, and *call on* Participants promptly to undertake further detailed work to, *inter alia*, establish the nature and extent of those disciplines, including transparency and enforceability. Appropriate and effective special and differential treatment for developing and least-developed Members should be an integral part of the fisheries subsidies negotiations, taking into account the importance of this sector to

development priorities, poverty reduction, and livelihood and food security concerns;

10.   *direct* the Group to intensify and accelerate the negotiating process in all areas of its mandate, on the basis of detailed textual proposals before the Group or yet to be submitted, and complete the process of analysing proposals by Participants on the AD and SCM Agreements as soon as possible;

11.   *mandate* the Chairman to prepare, early enough to assure a timely outcome within the context of the 2006 end date for the Doha Development Agenda and taking account of progress in other areas of the negotiations, consolidated texts of the AD and SCM Agreements that shall be the basis for the final stage of the negotiations.

II. Regional Trade Agreements

1.   We welcome the progress in negotiations to clarify and improve the WTO's disciplines and procedures on regional trade agreements (RTAs). Such agreements, which can foster trade liberalization and promote development, have become an important element in the trade policies of virtually all Members. Transparency of RTAs is thus of systemic interest as are disciplines that ensure the complementarity of RTAs with the WTO.

2.   We commend the progress in defining the elements of a transparency mechanism for RTAs, aimed, in particular, at improving existing WTO procedures for gathering factual information on RTAs, without prejudice to the rights and obligations of Members. We instruct the Negotiating Group on Rules to intensify its efforts to resolve outstanding issues, with a view to a provisional decision on RTA transparency by 30 April 2006.

3.   We also note with appreciation the work of the Negotiating Group on Rules on WTO's disciplines governing RTAs, including *inter alia* on the "substantially all the trade" requirement, the length of RTA transition periods and RTA developmental aspects. We instruct the Group to intensify negotiations, based on text proposals as soon as possible after the Sixth Ministerial Conference, so as to arrive at appropriate outcomes by end 2006.

Annex E

Trade Facilitation

Report by the Negotiating Group on Trade Facilitation to the TNC

1.   Since its establishment on 12 October 2004, the Negotiating Group on Trade Facilitation met eleven times to carry out work under the mandate contained in Annex D of the Decision adopted by the General Council on 1 August 2004. The negotiations are benefiting from the fact that the mandate allows for the central development dimension of the Doha negotiations to be addressed directly through the widely acknowledged benefits of trade facilitation reforms for all WTO Members, the enhancement of trade facilitation capacity in developing countries and LDCs, and provisions on special and differential treatment (S&DT) that provide flexibility. Based on the Group's Work Plan (TN/TF/1), Members contributed to the agreed agenda of the Group, tabling 60 written submissions sponsored by more than 100 delegations. Members appreciate the transparent and inclusive manner in which the negotiations are being conducted.

2.   Good progress has been made in all areas covered by the mandate, through both verbal and written contributions by Members. A considerable part of the Negotiating Group's meetings has been spent on addressing the negotiating objective of improving and clarifying relevant aspects of GATT Articles V, VIII and X, on which about 40 written submissions[1] have been tabled by Members representing the full spectrum of the WTO's Membership. Through discussions on these submissions and related questions and answers (JOB(05)/222), Members have advanced their understanding of the measures in question and are working towards common ground on many aspects of this part of the negotiating mandate. Many of these submissions also covered the negotiating objective of enhancing technical assistance and support for capacity building on trade facilitation, as well as the practical application of the principle of S&DT. The Group also discussed other valuable submissions dedicated to these issues.[2] Advances have also been made on the objective of arriving at provisions for effective cooperation between customs or any other appropriate authorities on trade facilitation and customs compliance issues, where two written proposals have been discussed.[3] Members have also made valuable contributions on the identification of trade facilitation needs and priorities, development aspects, cost implications and inter-agency cooperation.[4]

3.   Valuable input has been provided by a number of Members in the form of national experience papers[5] describing national trade facilitation reform processes. In appreciation of the value to developing countries and LDCs of this aspect of the negotiations, the

Negotiating Group recommends that Members be encouraged to continue this information sharing exercise.

4.　　　Building on the progress made in the negotiations so far, and with a view to developing a set of multilateral commitments on all elements of the mandate, the Negotiating Group recommends that it continue to intensify its negotiations on the basis of Members' proposals, as reflected currently in document TN/TF/W/43/Rev.4, and any new proposals to be presented. Without prejudice to individual Member's positions on individual proposals, a list of (I) proposed measures to improve and clarify GATT Articles V, VIII and X; (II) proposed provisions for effective cooperation between customs and other authorities on trade facilitation and customs compliance; and, (III) cross-cutting submissions; is provided below to facilitate further negotiations. In carrying out this work and in tabling further proposals, Members should be mindful of the overall deadline for finishing the negotiations and the resulting need to move into focussed drafting mode early enough after the Sixth Ministerial Conference so as to allow for a timely conclusion of text-based negotiations on all aspects of the mandate.

5.　　　Work needs to continue and broaden on the process of identifying individual Member's trade facilitation needs and priorities, and the cost implications of possible measures. The Negotiating Group recommends that relevant international organizations be invited to continue to assist Members in this process, recognizing the important contributions being made by them already, and be encouraged to continue and intensify their work more generally in support of the negotiations.

6.　　　In light of the vital importance of technical assistance and capacity building to allow developing countries and LDCs to fully participate in and benefit from the negotiations, the Negotiating Group recommends that the commitments in Annex D's mandate in this area be reaffirmed, reinforced and made operational in a timely manner. To bring the negotiations to a successful conclusion, special attention needs to be paid to support for technical assistance and capacity building that will allow developing counties and LDCs to participate effectively in the negotiations, and to technical assistance and capacity building to implement the results of the negotiations that is precise, effective and operational, and reflects the trade facilitation needs and priorities of developing countries and LDCs. Recognizing the valuable assistance already being provided in this area, the Negotiating Group recommends that Members, in particular developed ones, continue to intensify their support in a comprehensive manner and on a long-term and sustainable basis, backed by secure funding.

7.   The Negotiating Group also recommends that it deepen and intensify its negotiations on the issue of S&DT, with a view to arriving at S&DT provisions that are precise, effective and operational and that allow for necessary flexibility in implementing the results of the negotiations. Reaffirming the linkages among the elements of Annex D, the Negotiating Group recommends that further negotiations on S&DT build on input presented by Members in the context of measures related to GATT Articles V, VIII and X and in their proposals of a cross-cutting nature on S&DT.

Notes

[1] TN/TF/W/6-W/15, W/17-W/26, W/28, W/30-W32, W/34-36, W/38-W/40, W/42, W/44-W/49, W/53, W/55, W/58, W/60-W/62, W/64-W/67, W/69, W/70.

[2] TN/TF/W/33, W/41, W/56, W/63, W/73 and W/74.

[3] TN/TF/W/57 and W/68.

[4] TN/TF/W/29, W/33, W/41, W/62 and W/63.

[5] TN/TF/W/48, W/50 , W/53, W/55, W/58, W/60, W/61, W/65, W/69 and W/75.

I. PROPOSED MEASURES TO IMPROVE AND CLARIFY GATT ARTICLES V, VIII AND X

A. PUBLICATION AND AVAILABILITY OF INFORMATION

- Publication of Trade Regulations

- Publication of Penalty Provisions

- Internet Publication

  (a) of elements set out in Article X of GATT 1994

  (b) of specified information setting forth procedural sequence and other requirements for importing goods

- Notification of Trade Regulations

- Establishment of Enquiry Points/SNFP/Information Centres

- Other Measures to Enhance the Availability of Information

B. TIME PERIODS BETWEEN PUBLICATION AND IMPLEMENTATION

- Interval between Publication and Entry into Force

C. CONSULTATION AND COMMENTS ON NEW AND AMENDED RULES

- Prior Consultation and Commenting on New and Amended Rules

- Information on Policy Objectives Sought

D. ADVANCE RULINGS

- Provision of Advance Rulings

E. APPEAL PROCEDURES

- Right of Appeal

- Release of Goods in Event of Appeal

F. OTHER MEASURES TO ENHANCE IMPARTIALITY AND NON-DISCRIMINATION

- Uniform Administration of Trade Regulations

- Maintenance and Reinforcement of Integrity and Ethical Conduct Among Officials

(a) Establishment of a Code of Conduct

(b) Computerized System to Reduce/Eliminate Discretion

(c) System of Penalties

(d) Technical Assistance to Create/Build up Capacities to Prevent and Control Customs Offences

(e) Appointment of Staff for Education and Training

(f) Coordination and Control Mechanisms

G. FEES AND CHARGES CONNECTED WITH IMPORTATION AND EXPORTATION

- General Disciplines on Fees and Charges Imposed on or in Connection with Importation and Exportation

  (a) Specific Parameters for Fees/Charges

  (b) Publication/Notification of Fees/Charges

  (c) Prohibition of Collection of Unpublished Fees and Charges

  (d) Periodic Review of Fees/Charges

  (e) Automated Payment

- Reduction/Minimization of the Number and Diversity of Fees/Charges

H. FORMALITIES CONNECTED WITH IMPORTATION AND EXPORTATION

- Disciplines on Formalities/Procedures and Data/Documentation Requirements Connected with Importation and Exportation

  (a) Non-discrimination

  (b) Periodic Review of Formalities and Requirements

  (c) Reduction/Limitation of Formalities and Documentation Requirements

  (d) Use of International Standards

  (e) Uniform Customs Code

  (f) Acceptance of Commercially Available Information and of Copies

(g) Automation

(h) Single Window/One-time Submission

(i) Elimination of Pre-Shipment Inspection

(j) Phasing out Mandatory Use of Customs Brokers

I. CONSULARIZATION

- Prohibition of Consular Transaction Requirement

J. BORDER AGENCY COOPERATION

- Coordination of Activities and Requirement of all Border Agencies

K. RELEASE AND CLEARANCE OF GOODS

- Expedited/Simplified Release and Clearance of Goods

  (a) Pre-arrival Clearance

  (b) Expedited Procedures for Express Shipments

  (c) Risk Management /Analysis, Authorized Traders

  (d) Post-Clearance Audit

  (e) Separating Release from Clearance Procedures

  (f) Other Measures to Simplify Customs Release and Clearance

- Establishment and Publication of Average Release and Clearance Times

L. TARIFF CLASSIFICATION

- Objective Criteria for Tariff Classification

M. MATTERS RELATED TO GOODS TRANSIT

- Strengthened Non-discrimination

- Disciplines on Fees and Charges

  (a) Publication of Fees and Charges and Prohibition of Unpublished ones

  (b) Periodic Review of Fees and Charges

(a) More effective Disciplines on Charges for Transit

(b) Periodic Exchange Between Neighbouring Authorities

- Disciplines on Transit Formalities and Documentation Requirements

(a) Periodic Review

(b) Reduction/Simplification

(c) Harmonization/Standardization

(d) Promotion of Regional Transit Arrangements

(e) Simplified and Preferential Clearance for Certain Goods

(f) Limitation of Inspections and Controls

(g) Sealing

(h) Cooperation and Coordination on Document Requirements

(i) Monitoring

(j) Bonded Transport Regime/Guarantees

- Improved Coordination and Cooperation

(a) Amongst Authorities

(b) Between Authorities and the Private Sector

- Operationalization and Clarification of Terms

II. PROPOSED PROVISIONS FOR EFFECTIVE COOPERATION BETWEEN CUSTOMS AND OTHER AUTHORITIES ON TRADE FACILITATION AND CUSTOMS COMPLIANCE

- Multilateral Mechanism for the Exchange and Handling of Information

III. CROSS-CUTTING SUBMISSIONS

1. Needs and Priorities Identification

- General tool to assess needs and priorities and current levels of trade facilitation

- Take result of assessment as one basis for establishing trade facilitation rules, arranging S&D treatment and providing technical assistance and capacity building support

2. Technical Assistance and Capacity Building

- Technical Assistance and Capacity Building in the Course of the Negotiations

  - Identification of Needs and Priorities

  - Compilation of Needs and Priorities of Individual Members

  - Support for Clarification and Educative Process Including Training

- Technical Assistance and Capacity Building Beyond the Negotiations Phase

  - Implementation of the Outcome

  - Coordination Mechanisms for Implementing Needs and Priorities as well as Commitments

3. Multiple-Areas

  - Identification of Trade Facilitation Needs and Priorities of Members

  - Cost Assessment

  - Inter-Agency Cooperation

  - Links and Inter-relationship between the Elements of Annex D

  - Inventory of Trade Facilitation Measures

  - Assessment of the Current Situation

  - Timing and Sequencing of Measures

Annex F

Special and Differential Treatment
LDC Agreement-specific Proposals

23) Understanding in Respect of Waivers of Obligations under the GATT 1994

(i)   We agree that requests for waivers by least-developed country Members under Article IX of the WTO Agreement and the Understanding in respect of Waivers of Obligations under the GATT 1994 shall be given positive consideration and a decision taken within 60 days.

(ii)   When considering requests for waivers by other Members exclusively in favour of least-developed country Members, we agree that a decision shall be taken within 60 days, or in exceptional circumstances as expeditiously as possible thereafter, without prejudice to the rights of other Members.

36) Decision on Measures in Favour of Least-Developed Countries

We agree that developed-country Members shall, and developing-country Members declaring themselves in a position to do so should:

(a) (i) Provide duty-free and quota-free market access on a lasting basis, for all products originating from all LDCs by 2008 or no later than the start of the implementation period in a manner that ensures stability, security and predictability.

(ii) Members facing difficulties at this time to provide market access as set out above shall provide duty-free and quota-free market access for at least 97 per cent of products originating from LDCs, defined at the tariff line level, by 2008 or no later than the start of the implementation period. In addition, these Members shall take steps to progressively achieve compliance with the obligations set out above, taking into account the impact on other developing countries at similar levels of development, and, as appropriate, by incrementally building on the initial list of covered products.

(iii) Developing-country Members shall be permitted to phase in their commitments and shall enjoy appropriate flexibility in coverage.

(b) Ensure that preferential rules of origin applicable to imports from LDCs are transparent and simple, and contribute to facilitating market access.

Members shall notify the implementation of the schemes adopted under this decision every year to the Committee on Trade and Development. The Committee on Trade and Development shall annually review the steps taken to provide duty-free and quota-free market access to the LDCs and report to the General Council for appropriate action.

We urge all donors and relevant international institutions to increase financial and technical support aimed at the diversification of LDC economies, while providing additional financial and technical assistance through appropriate delivery mechanisms to meet their implementation obligations, including fulfilling SPS and TBT requirements, and to assist them in managing their adjustment processes, including those necessary to face the results of MFN multilateral trade liberalisation.

38) Decision on Measures in Favour of Least-Developed Countries

It is reaffirmed that least-developed country Members will only be required to undertake commitments and concessions to the extent consistent with their individual development, financial or trade needs, or their administrative and institutional capacities.

Within the context of coherence arrangements with other international institutions, we urge donors, multilateral agencies and international financial institutions to coordinate their work to ensure that LDCs are not subjected to conditionalities on loans, grants and official development assistance that are inconsistent with their rights and obligations under the WTO Agreements.

84) Agreement on Trade-Related Investment Measures

LDCs shall be allowed to maintain on a temporary basis existing measures that deviate from their obligations under the TRIMs Agreement. For this purpose, LDCs shall notify the Council for Trade in Goods (CTG) of such measures within two years, starting 30 days after the date of this declaration. LDCs will be allowed to maintain these existing measures until the end of a new transition period, lasting seven years. This transition period may be extended by the CTG under the existing procedures set out in the TRIMs Agreement, taking into account the individual financial, trade, and development needs of the Member in question.

LDCs shall also be allowed to introduce new measures that deviate from their obligations under the TRIMs Agreement. These new TRIMs shall be notified to the CTG no later than six months after their adoption. The CTG shall give positive consideration to such notifications, taking into account the individual financial, trade, and development needs of the Member in question. The duration of these measures will not exceed five years, renewable subject to review and decision by the CTG.

Any measures incompatible with the TRIMs Agreement and adopted under this decision shall be phased out by year 2020.

88) Decision on Measures in Favour of Least-Developed Countries - Paragraph 1

Least-developed country Members, whilst reaffirming their commitment to the fundamental principles of the WTO and relevant provisions of GATT 1994, and while complying with the general rules set out in the aforesaid instruments, will only be required to undertake commitments and concessions to the extent consistent with their individual development, financial and trade needs, and their administrative and institutional capabilities. Should a least-developed country Member find that it is not in a position to comply with a specific obligation or commitment on these grounds, it shall bring the matter to the attention of the General Council for examination and appropriate action.

We agree that the implementation by LDCs of their obligations or commitments will require further technical and financial support directly related to the nature and scope of such obligations or commitments, and direct the WTO to coordinate its efforts with donors and relevant agencies to significantly increase aid for trade-related technical assistance and capacity building.

Trade Related Aspects of Intellectual Property Rights (TRIPS) and public health

- 2002 decision on least-developed countries
- 2003 decision on compulsory licensing for export

Geneva: Director-General Supachai Panitchpakdi, who was in office when members agreed on the 2003 decision on intellectual property and public health.

TRIPS Council decision allowing least-developed countries until 2016 to protect pharmaceutical patents and test data

A few days after this was agreed in the TRIPS Council, the General Council reached a closely related decision on 8 July 2002 (WT/L/478), allowing least-developed countries until 2016 to grant exclusive marketing rights under Article 70.9 of the TRIPS Agreement. This deals with the situation where pharmaceutical patents are not protected, but a patent application has been submitted and the government has allowed the product to be marketed.

IP/C/25
1 July 2002
(02-3664)

**Council for Trade-Related Aspects
of Intellectual Property Rights**

EXTENSION OF THE TRANSITION PERIOD UNDER ARTICLE 66.1 OF THE TRIPS AGREEMENT FOR LEAST-DEVELOPED COUNTRY MEMBERS FOR CERTAIN OBLIGATIONS WITH RESPECT TO PHARMACEUTICAL PRODUCTS

Decision of the Council for TRIPS of 27 June 2002

The Council for Trade-Related Aspects of Intellectual Property Rights (the "Council for TRIPS"),

Having regard to paragraph 1 of Article 66 of the TRIPS Agreement;

Having regard to the instruction of the Ministerial Conference to the Council for TRIPS contained in paragraph 7 of the Declaration on the TRIPS Agreement and Public Health (WT/MIN(01)/DEC/2) (the "Declaration");

Considering that paragraph 7 of the Declaration constitutes a duly motivated request by the least-developed country Members for an extension of the period under paragraph 1 of Article 66 of the TRIPS Agreement;

Decides as follows:

1.   Least-developed country Members will not be obliged, with respect to pharmaceutical products, to implement or apply Sections 5 and 7 of Part II of the TRIPS Agreement or to enforce rights provided for under these Sections until 1 January 2016.

2.   This decision is made without prejudice to the right of least-developed country Members to seek other extensions of the period provided for in paragraph 1 of Article 66 of the TRIPS Agreement.

General Council decision on compulsory licensing for export ('Paragraph 6')

The General Council has adopted two decisions on the "Paragraph 6" system - a reference to Paragraph 6 of the Doha Ministerial Declaration on TRIPS and Public Health. The decisions dealt with an obstacle for countries needing to import cheaper generics made under compulsory licensing when they were unable to manufacture the medicines themselves. Now, pharmaceutical products can be made under compulsory licence in one country, exclusively for exporting to another country which lacks its own production capacity, provided certain conditions are met.

The first decision, adopted in 2003 just before the Cancún Ministerial Conference, is reproduced here. It is the one that is currently in force, a waiver bypassing provisions of Articles 31(f) and 31(h) of the TRIPS Agreement. The second (General Council decision WT/L/641) was adopted in 2005 on the eve of the Hong Kong Ministerial Conference. It will replace the waiver with a permanent amendment whose contents are identical, when two thirds of the WTO's members have accepted the change.

When the waiver and the proposed amendment were adopted, the General Council chairperson also read out a statement, which can be found on the WTO website, along with other information on the subject, at http://www.wto.org/trips.

WT/L/540 and Corr.1
2 September 2003
(03-4582)

IMPLEMENTATION OF PARAGRAPH 6 OF THE DOHA DECLARATION ON THE TRIPS AGREEMENT AND PUBLIC HEALTH
Decision of 30 August 2003 ·

The General Council,

Having regard to paragraphs 1, 3 and 4 of Article IX of the Marrakesh Agreement Establishing the World Trade Organization ("the WTO Agreement");

· *Secretariat note for information purposes only and without prejudice to Members' legal rights and obligations:* This Decision was adopted by the General Council in the light of a statement read out by the Chairman, which can be found in JOB(03)/177. This statement will be reproduced in the minutes of the General Council to be issued as WT/GC/M/82.

Conducting the functions of the Ministerial Conference in the interval between meetings pursuant to paragraph 2 of Article IV of the WTO Agreement;

Noting the Declaration on the TRIPS Agreement and Public Health (WT/MIN(01)/DEC/2) (the "Declaration") and, in particular, the instruction of the Ministerial Conference to the Council for TRIPS contained in paragraph 6 of the Declaration to find an expeditious solution to the problem of the difficulties that WTO Members with insufficient or no manufacturing capacities in the pharmaceutical sector could face in making effective use of compulsory licensing under the TRIPS Agreement and to report to the General Council before the end of 2002;

Recognizing, where eligible importing Members seek to obtain supplies under the system set out in this Decision, the importance of a rapid response to those needs consistent with the provisions of this Decision;

Noting that, in the light of the foregoing, exceptional circumstances exist justifying waivers from the obligations set out in paragraphs (f) and (h) of Article 31 of the TRIPS Agreement with respect to pharmaceutical products;

Decides as follows:

1. For the purposes of this Decision:

    (a) "pharmaceutical product" means any patented product, or product manufactured through a patented process, of the pharmaceutical sector needed to address the public health problems as recognized in paragraph 1 of the Declaration. It is understood that active ingredients necessary for its manufacture and diagnostic kits needed for its use would be included[1];

    (b) "eligible importing Member" means any least-developed country Member, and any other Member that has made a notification[2] to the Council for TRIPS of its intention to use the system as an importer, it being understood that a Member may notify at any time that it will use the system in whole or in a limited way, for example only in the case of a national emergency or other circumstances of extreme urgency or in cases of public non-commercial use. It is noted that some Members will not use the system set out in this Decision as importing Members[3] and that some other Members have stated that, if they use the system, it would be in no more than situations of national emergency or other circumstances of extreme urgency;

(c)   "exporting Member" means a Member using the system set out in this Decision to produce pharmaceutical products for, and export them to, an eligible importing Member.

2.   The obligations of an exporting Member under Article 31(f) of the TRIPS Agreement shall be waived with respect to the grant by it of a compulsory licence to the extent necessary for the purposes of production of a pharmaceutical product(s) and its export to an eligible importing Member(s) in accordance with the terms set out below in this paragraph:

(a)   the eligible importing Member(s)[4] has made a notification[2] to the Council for TRIPS, that:

    (i)   specifies the names and expected quantities of the product(s) needed[5];

    (ii)   confirms that the eligible importing Member in question, other than a least-developed country Member, has established that it has insufficient or no manufacturing capacities in the pharmaceutical sector for the product(s) in question in one of the ways set out in the Annex to this Decision; and

    (iii)   confirms that, where a pharmaceutical product is patented in its territory, it has granted or intends to grant a compulsory licence in accordance with Article 31 of the TRIPS Agreement and the provisions of this Decision[6];

(b)   the compulsory licence issued by the exporting Member under this Decision shall contain the following conditions:

    (i)   only the amount necessary to meet the needs of the eligible importing Member(s) may be manufactured under the licence and the entirety of this production shall be exported to the Member(s) which has notified its needs to the Council for TRIPS;

    (ii)   products produced under the licence shall be clearly identified as being produced under the system set out in this Decision through specific labelling or marking. Suppliers should distinguish such products through special packaging and/or special colouring/shaping of the products themselves, provided that such distinction is feasible and does not have a significant impact on price; and

(iii)   before shipment begins, the licensee shall post on a website[7] the following information:

- the quantities being supplied to each destination as referred to in indent (i) above; and

- the distinguishing features of the product(s) referred to in indent (ii) above;

(c)   the exporting Member shall notify[8] the Council for TRIPS of the grant of the licence, including the conditions attached to it.[9] The information provided shall include the name and address of the licensee, the product(s) for which the licence has been granted, the quantity(ies) for which it has been granted, the country(ies) to which the product(s) is (are) to be supplied and the duration of the licence. The notification shall also indicate the address of the website referred to in subparagraph (b)(iii) above.

3.   Where a compulsory licence is granted by an exporting Member under the system set out in this Decision, adequate remuneration pursuant to Article 31(h) of the TRIPS Agreement shall be paid in that Member taking into account the economic value to the importing Member of the use that has been authorized in the exporting Member. Where a compulsory licence is granted for the same products in the eligible importing Member, the obligation of that Member under Article 31(h) shall be waived in respect of those products for which remuneration in accordance with the first sentence of this paragraph is paid in the exporting Member.

4.   In order to ensure that the products imported under the system set out in this Decision are used for the public health purposes underlying their importation, eligible importing Members shall take reasonable measures within their means, proportionate to their administrative capacities and to the risk of trade diversion to prevent re-exportation of the products that have actually been imported into their territories under the system. In the event that an eligible importing Member that is a developing country Member or a least-developed country Member experiences difficulty in implementing this provision, developed country Members shall provide, on request and on mutually agreed terms and conditions, technical and financial cooperation in order to facilitate its implementation.

5.   Members shall ensure the availability of effective legal means to prevent the importation into, and sale in, their territories of products produced under the system set out in this Decision and diverted to their markets inconsistently with its provisions, using the means already required to be available under the TRIPS Agreement. If any Member considers

that such measures are proving insufficient for this purpose, the matter may be reviewed in the Council for TRIPS at the request of that Member.

6.   With a view to harnessing economies of scale for the purposes of enhancing purchasing power for, and facilitating the local production of, pharmaceutical products:

(i)   where a developing or least-developed country WTO Member is a party to a regional trade agreement within the meaning of Article XXIV of the GATT 1994 and the Decision of 28 November 1979 on Differential and More Favourable Treatment Reciprocity and Fuller Participation of Developing Countries (L/4903), at least half of the current membership of which is made up of countries presently on the United Nations list of least-developed countries, the obligation of that Member under Article 31(f) of the TRIPS Agreement shall be waived to the extent necessary to enable a pharmaceutical product produced or imported under a compulsory licence in that Member to be exported to the markets of those other developing or least-developed country parties to the regional trade agreement that share the health problem in question. It is understood that this will not prejudice the territorial nature of the patent rights in question;

(ii)   it is recognized that the development of systems providing for the grant of regional patents to be applicable in the above Members should be promoted. To this end, developed country Members undertake to provide technical cooperation in accordance with Article 67 of the TRIPS Agreement, including in conjunction with other relevant intergovernmental organizations.

7.   Members recognize the desirability of promoting the transfer of technology and capacity building in the pharmaceutical sector in order to overcome the problem identified in paragraph 6 of the Declaration. To this end, eligible importing Members and exporting Members are encouraged to use the system set out in this Decision in a way which would promote this objective. Members undertake to cooperate in paying special attention to the transfer of technology and capacity building in the pharmaceutical sector in the work to be undertaken pursuant to Article 66.2 of the TRIPS Agreement, paragraph 7 of the Declaration and any other relevant work of the Council for TRIPS.

8.   The Council for TRIPS shall review annually the functioning of the system set out in this Decision with a view to ensuring its effective operation and shall annually report

on its operation to the General Council. This review shall be deemed to fulfil the review requirements of Article IX:4 of the WTO Agreement.

9.   This Decision is without prejudice to the rights, obligations and flexibilities that Members have under the provisions of the TRIPS Agreement other than paragraphs (f) and (h) of Article 31, including those reaffirmed by the Declaration, and to their interpretation. It is also without prejudice to the extent to which pharmaceutical products produced under a compulsory licence can be exported under the present provisions of Article 31(f) of the TRIPS Agreement.

10.   Members shall not challenge any measures taken in conformity with the provisions of the waivers contained in this Decision under subparagraphs 1(b) and 1(c) of Article XXIII of GATT 1994.

11.   This Decision, including the waivers granted in it, shall terminate for each Member on the date on which an amendment to the TRIPS Agreement replacing its provisions takes effect for that Member. The TRIPS Council shall initiate by the end of 2003 work on the preparation of such an amendment with a view to its adoption within six months, on the understanding that the amendment will be based, where appropriate, on this Decision and on the further understanding that it will not be part of the negotiations referred to in paragraph 45 of the Doha Ministerial Declaration (WT/MIN(01)/DEC/1).

Notes

[1] This subparagraph is without prejudice to subparagraph 1(b).

[2] It is understood that this notification does not need to be approved by a WTO body in order to use the system set out in this Decision.

[3] Australia, Austria, Belgium, Canada, Denmark, Finland, France, Germany, Greece, Iceland, Ireland, Italy, Japan, Luxembourg, the Netherlands, New Zealand, Norway, Portugal, Spain, Sweden, Switzerland, the United Kingdom and the United States.

[4] Joint notifications providing the information required under this subparagraph may be made by the regional organizations referred to in paragraph 6 of this Decision on behalf of eligible importing Members using the system that are parties to them, with the agreement of those parties.

[5] The notification will be made available publicly by the WTO Secretariat through a page on the WTO website dedicated to this Decision.

[6] This subparagraph is without prejudice to Article 66.1 of the TRIPS Agreement.

[7] The licensee may use for this purpose its own website or, with the assistance of the WTO Secretariat, the page on the WTO website dedicated to this Decision.

[8] It is understood that this notification does not need to be approved by a WTO body in order to use the system set out in this Decision.

[9] The notification will be made available publicly by the WTO Secretariat through a page on the WTO website dedicated to this Decision.

ANNEX
Assessment of Manufacturing Capacities in the Pharmaceutical Sector

Least-developed country Members are deemed to have insufficient or no manufacturing capacities in the pharmaceutical sector.

For other eligible importing Members insufficient or no manufacturing capacities for the product(s) in question may be established in either of the following ways:

(i) the Member in question has established that it has no manufacturing capacity in the pharmaceutical sector;

OR

(ii) where the Member has some manufacturing capacity in this sector, it has examined this capacity and found that, excluding any capacity owned or controlled by the patent owner, it is currently insufficient for the purposes of meeting its needs. When it is established that such capacity has become sufficient to meet the Member's needs, the system shall no longer apply.

Photo credits:
Cover photo: WTO/Jay Louvion.
Pages 2-3, 72 (inset bottom right): Denis Balibouse.
Pages 20, 64, 72, 162: WTO .
Page 8: Peter Ungphakorn.